教育部、国家语委重大文化工程
　　"中华思想文化术语传播工程"成果
国家社会科学基金重大项目
　　"中国核心术语国际影响力研究"（21&ZD158）
"十四五"国家重点出版物出版规划项目
获评第二届向全国推荐中华优秀传统文化普及图书

典藏版·第一卷

Key Concepts in Chinese Thought and Culture
中华思想文化术语 1

《中华思想文化术语》编委会 编

外语教学与研究出版社
FOREIGN LANGUAGE TEACHING AND RESEARCH PRESS
北京 BEIJING

图书在版编目（CIP）数据

中华思想文化术语：典藏版. 第一卷. 1：汉英对照 /《中华思想文化术语》编委会编. —— 北京：外语教学与研究出版社，2023.12
ISBN 978-7-5213-4878-1

Ⅰ. ①中… Ⅱ. ①中… Ⅲ. ①中华文化－术语－汉、英 Ⅳ. ①K203-61

中国国家版本馆 CIP 数据核字 (2023) 第 205208 号

出 版 人　王　芳
项目策划　刘旭璐
责任编辑　赵璞玉
责任校对　王海燕
封面设计　梧桐影
版式设计　孙莉明
出版发行　外语教学与研究出版社
社　　址　北京市西三环北路 19 号（100089）
网　　址　https://www.fltrp.com
印　　刷　三河市北燕印装有限公司
开　　本　710×1000　1/16
印　　张　57
版　　次　2024 年 1 月第 1 版 2024 年 1 月第 1 次印刷
书　　号　ISBN 978-7-5213-4878-1
定　　价　349.00 元（全五册）

如有图书采购需求，图书内容或印刷装订等问题，侵权、盗版书籍等线索，请拨打以下电话或关注官方服务号：
客服电话：400 898 7008
官方服务号：微信搜索并关注公众号"外研社官方服务号"
外研社购书网址：https://fltrp.tmall.com

物料号：348780001

"中华思想文化术语传播工程"专家团队
(按音序)

Scholars Participating in the Project "Key Concepts in Chinese Thought and Culture: Communication Through Translation"

顾问（Advisors）

李学勤（Li Xueqin）　　　　林戊荪（Lin Wusun）
叶嘉莹（Florence Chia-ying Yeh）　张岂之（Zhang Qizhi）
楼宇烈（Lou Yulie）　　　　王　宁（Wang Ning）

专家委员会（Committee of Scholars）

主任（Director）

韩　震（Han Zhen）

委员（Members）

晁福林（Chao Fulin）　　　　陈德彰（Chen Dezhang）
陈明明（Chen Mingming）　　冯志伟（Feng Zhiwei）
韩经太（Han Jingtai）　　　　黄友义（Huang Youyi）
金元浦（Jin Yuanpu）　　　　静　炜（Jing Wei）
李建中（Li Jianzhong）　　　李雪涛（Li Xuetao）
李照国（Li Zhaoguo）　　　　聂长顺（Nie Changshun）
潘公凯（Pan Gongkai）　　　王　博（Wang Bo）

王柯平（Wang Keping）　　叶　朗（Ye Lang）
袁济喜（Yuan Jixi）　　袁行霈（Yuan Xingpei）
张　晶（Zhang Jing）　　张立文（Zhang Liwen）
张西平（Zhang Xiping）　　郑述谱（Zheng Shupu）

特邀汉学家（Scholars of China Studies）

艾　恺（Guy Salvatore Alitto）　　安乐哲（Roger T. Ames）
白罗米（Luminiţa Bălan）　　包华石（Martin Joseph Powers）
陈瑞河（Madaras Réka）　　狄伯杰（B. R. Deepak）
顾　彬（Wolfgang Kubin）　　韩安德（Harry Anders Hansson）
韩　裴（Petko Todorov Hinov）　　柯鸿冈（Paul Crook）
柯马凯（Michael Crook）　　斯巴修（Iljaz Spahiu）
王健、李盈（Jan & Yvonne Walls）　　魏查理（Charles Willemen）

学术委员会（Academic Committee）

白振奎（Bai Zhenkui）　　蔡力坚（Cai Lijian）
曹轩梓（Cao Xuanzi）　　陈海燕（Chen Haiyan）
陈少明（Chen Shaoming）　　程景牧（Cheng Jingmu）
丁　浩（Ding Hao）　　付志斌（Fu Zhibin）
干春松（Gan Chunsong）　　郭晓东（Guo Xiaodong）
韩志华（Han Zhihua）　　何　淼（He Miao）
何世剑（He Shijian）　　胡　海（Hu Hai）
贾德忠（Jia Dezhong）　　姜海龙（Jiang Hailong）
柯修文（Daniel Canaris）　　黎　臻（Li Zhen）

李存山（Li Cunshan）	李恭忠（Li Gongzhong）
李景林（Li Jinglin）	林敏洁（Lin Minjie）
林少阳（Lin Shaoyang）	刘　佳（Liu Jia）
刘　璐（Liu Lu）	刘　青（Liu Qing）
吕玉华（Lü Yuhua）	梅缵月（Mei Zuanyue）
孟庆楠（Meng Qingnan）	裴德思（Thorsten Pattberg）
彭冬林（Peng Donglin）	乔　希（Joshua Mason）
任大援（Ren Dayuan）	邵亦鹏（Shao Yipeng）
沈卫星（Shen Weixing）	施晓菁（Lynette Shi）
陶黎庆（Tao Liqing）	童孝华（Tong Xiaohua）
王丽丽（Wang Lili）	王　琳（Wang Lin）
王明杰（Wang Mingjie）	王维东（Wang Weidong）
王　鑫（Wang Xin）	温海明（Wen Haiming）
吴根友（Wu Genyou）	吴礼敬（Wu Lijing）
夏　晶（Xia Jing）	谢远笋（Xie Yuansun）
辛红娟（Xin Hongjuan）	徐明强（Xu Mingqiang）
徐亚男（Xu Yanan）	许家星（Xu Jiaxing）
严学军（Yan Xuejun）	张　静（Zhang Jing）
张子尧（Zhang Ziyao）	章思英（Zhang Siying）
章伟文（Zhang Weiwen）	赵　桐（Zhao Tong）
赵　悠（Zhao You）	郑　开（Zheng Kai）
周云帆（Zhou Yunfan）	朱绩崧（Zhu Jisong）
朱良志（Zhu Liangzhi）	朱　渊（Zhu Yuan）
左　励（Zuo Li）	

前言

"中华思想文化术语"的定义可以表述为：由中华民族所创造或构建，凝聚、浓缩了中华哲学思想、人文精神、思维方式、价值观念，以词或短语形式固化的概念和文化核心词。它们是中华民族几千年来对自然与社会进行探索和理性思索的成果，积淀着中华民族的历史智慧，反映中华民族最深沉的精神追求以及理性思索的深度与广度；其所蕴含的人文思想、思维方式、价值观念已经作为一种"生命基因"深深融于中华子孙的血液，内化为中华民族共同的性格和信仰，并由此支撑起中华数千年的学术传统、思想文化和精神世界。它是当代中国人理解中国古代哲学思想、人文精神、思维方式、价值观念之变化乃至文学艺术、历史等各领域发展的核心关键，也是世界其他国家和民族了解当代中国、中华民族和海外华人之精神世界的钥匙。

当今世界已进入文化多元与话语多极时代。世界不同区域、不同国家、不同民族的文明，其流动融合之快、之广、之深超过历史任何时期。每个国家和民族都有自己独具的思想文化和话语体系，都应在世界文明、世界话语体系中占有一席之地，得到它应有的地位和尊重。而思想文化术语无疑是一个国家和民族话语体系中最核心、最本质的部分，是它的思想之"髓"、文化之"根"、精神之"魂"、学术之"核"。越来越多的有识之士认识到，中华思想文化蕴藏着解决当今人类所面临的许多难题的重要启示，中华民族所倡导的"厚德载物""道法自然""天人合一""和而不同""民惟邦本""经世致用"等思想，以及它所追求的"协和万邦""天下一家"、世界"大同"，代表了当今世界文明的发展趋势，也因此成为国际社会的共识。越来越多的外国学者和友人对中华思想文化及其术语产生浓厚的兴趣，希望有更全面、更进一步的了解。

今天我们整理、诠释、翻译、传播中华思想文化术语，目的是立足于中华思想文化，通过全面系统的整理与诠释，深度挖掘其中既能反映中华哲学思想、人文精神、思维方式、价值观念、文化特征，又具跨越时空、超越国度之意义，以及富有永恒魅力与当代价值的含义和内容，并将其译成英语等语言，让世界更客观、更全面地认识中国，了解中华民族的过去和现在，了解当代中国人及海外华人的精神世界，从而推动国家间的平等对话及不同文明间的交流借鉴。

中华思想文化术语的整理、诠释和英语翻译得到了中国教育部、中国国际出版集团、中央编译局、北京大学、中国人民大学、武汉大学、北京外国语大学等单位的大力支持，得到了叶嘉莹、李学勤、张岂之、林戊荪、楼宇烈、王宁等海内外众多知名学者的支持。需要说明的是，"中华思想文化术语"这个概念是首次提出，其内涵和外延还有待学界更深入的研究；而且，如此大规模地整理、诠释、翻译中华思想文化术语，在中国也是首次，无成例可循。因此，我们的诠释与翻译一定还有待完善的地方，我们会及时吸纳广大读者的意见，不断提高术语诠释与翻译的质量。

2021年12月11日

Foreword

By "key concepts in Chinese thought and culture" we mean concepts and keywords or phrases the Chinese people have created or come to use and that are fundamentally pertinent to Chinese philosophy, humanistic spirit, way of thinking, and values. They represent the Chinese people's exploration of and rational thinking about nature and society over thousands of years. These concepts and expressions reflect the Chinese people's wisdom, their profound spiritual pursuit, as well as the depth and width of their thinking. Their way of thinking, values, and philosophy embodied in these concepts have become a kind of "life gene" in Chinese culture, and have long crystallized into the common personality and beliefs of the Chinese nation. For the Chinese people today, they serve as a key to a better understanding of the evolutions of their ancient philosophy, humanistic spirit, way of thinking, and values as well as the development of Chinese literature, art, and history. For people in other countries, these concepts open the door to understanding the spiritual world of contemporary China and the Chinese people, including those living overseas.

In the era of cultural diversity and multipolar discourse today, cultures of different countries and civilizations of different peoples are integrating faster, in greater depth, and on a greater scope than ever before. All countries and peoples have their own systems of thought, culture, and discourse, which should all have their place in the civilization and discourse systems of the world. They all deserve due respect. The concepts in thought and culture of a country and its people are naturally the most essential part of their discourse. They constitute the marrow of a nation's thought, the root of its culture, the soul of its spirit, and the core of its scholarship. More and more people of vision have come to recognize the inspirations Chinese thought and culture might offer to help resolve many difficult problems faced by mankind. The Chinese hold that a man should "have ample virtue and carry all things," "Dao operates naturally," "heaven and man are united as one," a man of virtue seeks "harmony but not uniformity," "people are the foundation of the state," and "study of ancient classics should meet present needs." The Chinese ideals such as "coexistence of all in harmony," "all the people under heaven are one family," and a world of "universal harmony" are drawing increasing attention among the international community. More and more international scholars and friends have become interested in learning and better understanding Chinese thought and culture in general, and the relevant concepts in particular.

In selecting, explaining, translating, and sharing concepts in Chinese thought and culture, we have adopted a comprehensive and systematic approach. Most of them not only reflect the characteristics of Chinese philosophy, humanistic spirit, way of thinking, values, and culture, but also have significance and/or implications that transcend time and national boundaries, and that still fascinate present-day readers and offer them food for thought. It is hoped that the translation of these concepts into English and other languages will help people in other countries to gain a more objective and more rounded understanding of China, of its people, of its past and present, and of the spiritual world of contemporary Chinese. Such understanding should be conducive to promoting equal dialogue between China and other countries and exchanges between different civilizations.

The selection, explanation, and translation of these concepts have been made possible thanks to the support of the Ministry of Education, China International Publishing Group, the Central Compilation and Translation Bureau, Peking University, Renmin University of China, Wuhan University, and Beijing Foreign Studies University, as well as the support of renowned scholars in China and abroad, including Florence Chia-ying Yeh, Li Xueqin, Zhang Qizhi, Lin Wusun, Lou Yulie, and Wang Ning.

The idea of compiling key concepts in Chinese thought and culture represents an innovation and the project calls much research and effort both in connotation and denotation. Furthermore, an endeavor like this has not been previously attempted on such a large scale. Lack of precedents means there must remain much room for improvement. Therefore, we welcome comments from all readers in the hope of better fulfilling this task.

December 11, 2021

目录
Contents

1. bēikǎi 悲慨
   Depressed and Enraged 1
2. běnmò 本末
   Ben and *Mo* (The Fundamental and the Incidental) 2
3. bōrě 般若
   Prajna / Wisdom 4
4. bù xué《shī》, wú yǐ yán 不学《诗》，无以言
   You Won't Be Able to Talk Properly with Others Without Studying *The Book of Songs.* 5
5. chéng 诚
   Sincerity 6
6. dàtóng 大同
   Universal Harmony 7
7. dào 道
   Dao (Way) 9
8. dé 德
   De (Virtue) 10
9. fāfèn-zhùshū 发愤著书
   Indignation Spurs One to Write Great Works. 11
10. fǎzhì 法治
    Rule by Law 13

11	fēng-yǎ-sòng 风雅颂	
	Ballad, Court Hymn, and Eulogy	14
12	fēngjiàn 封建	
	Feudal System / Feudalism	16
13	fěngyù 讽谕	
	Subtle Admonition	17
14	fù-bǐ-xìng 赋比兴	
	Narrative, Analogy, and Association	19
15	gédiào 格调	
	Form and Melody	20
16	huáxià 华夏	
	Huaxia / The Han People	22
17	huáiyuǎn-yǐdé 怀远以德	
	Embrace Distant Peoples by Means of Virtue	23
18	jīlǐ 肌理	
	Reasoning and Structure	24
19	jiāngshān 江山	
	Rivers and Mountains / Country or State Power	27
20	jiàohuà 教化	
	Shaping the Mind Through Education	27
21	jiǔzhōu 九州	
	Nine *Zhou* (Regions)	28

22 kējǔ 科举
   The Imperial Civil Examination System 30

23 lài yǔ Xīshī, dào tōng wéi yī 厉与西施，道通为一
   A Scabby Person and the Beautiful Lady Xishi Are the Same in the
   Eyes of Dao. 32

24 lè ér bù yín, āi ér bù shāng 乐而不淫，哀而不伤
   Express Enjoyment Without Indulgence and Express Grief
   Without Excessive Distress 33

25 lǐ 理
   Li 35

26 lìyòng-hòushēng 利用厚生
   Make Full Use of Resources to Enrich the People 36

27 liángshǐ 良史
   Trustworthy Historian / Factual History 37

28 liángzhī 良知
   Liangzhi (Conscience) 38

29 liùjīng jiē shǐ 六经皆史
   The Six Confucian Classics Are All About History. 39

30 liùyì 六义
   The Six Basic Elements 40

31 měicì 美刺
   Extolment and Satirical Criticism 42

32 mínwéibāngběn 民惟邦本
    People Are the Foundation of the State..................................44

33 qì 气
    Qi (Vital Force) 45

34 qíng 情
    Qing...46

35 qíngjǐng 情景
    Sentiment and Scenery 47

36 qù 趣
    Qu 49

37 rénwén-huàchéng 人文化成
    Edify the Populace to Achieve a Harmonious Society 50

38 rénzhì 人治
    Rule by Man 51

39 rén 仁
    Ren (Benevolence) 53

40 rìxīn 日新
    Constant Renewal 54

41 róngcái 镕裁
    Refining and Deleting 55

42 shèjì 社稷
    Gods of the Earth and the Five Grains / State / State Power...............57

43 shén 神
   Shen (Spirit / Spiritual) 58

44 shénsī 神思
   Imaginative Contemplation 60

45 shēng yī wú tīng, wù yī wú wén 声一无听，物一无文
   A Single Note Does Not Compose a Melodious Tune, Nor Does a
   Single Color Make a Beautiful Pattern. 61

46 shèng 圣
   Sage / Sageness 62

47 shī yán zhì 诗言志
   Poetry Expresses Aspirations. 63

48 shī yuán qíng 诗缘情
   Poetry Springs from Emotions. 64

49 shǐcái-sāncháng 史才三长
   Three Strengths of a Good Historian 66

50 shūyuàn 书院
   Classical Academy 67

51 shùntiān-yìngrén 顺天应人
   Follow the Mandate of Heaven and Comply with the Wishes of
   the People 69

52 tàijí 太极
   Taiji (The Supreme Ultimate) 70

53 tàixué 太学
Imperial Academy 71

54 tǐxìng 体性
Style and Temperament.. 72

55 tǐyòng 体用
Ti and *Yong*... 75

56 tiān 天
Tian (Heaven)... 76

57 tiānxià 天下
Tianxia (All Under Heaven) 77

58 wáng 王
King 78

59 wángdào 王道
Kingly Way (Benevolent Governance) 79

60 wéizhèng-yǐdé 为政以德
Governance Based on Virtue.. 81

61 wénmíng 文明
Wenming (Civilization) 82

62 wénqì 文气
Wenqi 83

63 wényǐzàidào 文以载道
Literature Is the Vehicle of Ideas. 84

64	wúwéi 无为 Non-action	86
65	wǔxíng 五行 *Wuxing*	87
66	wù 物 *Wu* (Thing / Matter)	89
67	xiàng wài zhī xiàng, jǐng wài zhī jǐng 象外之象，景外之景 The Image Beyond an Image, the Scene Beyond a Scene	90
68	xiéhé-wànbāng 协和万邦 Coexistence of All in Harmony	91
69	xīn 心 Heart / Mind	92
70	xìn yán bù měi, měi yán bù xìn 信言不美，美言不信 Trustworthy Words May Not Be Fine-sounding; Fine-sounding Words May Not Be Trustworthy.	94
71	xìng-guān-qún-yuàn 兴观群怨 Stimulation, Contemplation, Communication, and Criticism	95
72	xìngxiàng 兴象 *Xingxiang* (Inspiring Imagery)	97
73	xìng 性 *Xing* (Nature)	98
74	xìnglíng 性灵 *Xingling* (Inner Self)	100

75　xiū-qí-zhì-píng 修齐治平
　　Self-cultivation, Family Regulation, State Governance,
　　Bringing Peace to All Under Heaven 101

76　xū 虚
　　Xu (Void) 102

77　xūjìng 虚静
　　Void and Peace 103

78　xuánlǎn 玄览
　　Xuanlan (Pure-minded Contemplation) 105

79　xuǎnjǔ 选举
　　Select and Recommend 106

80　yǎsú 雅俗
　　Highbrow and Lowbrow 107

81　yǎngqì 养气
　　Cultivate *Qi* 109

82　yī 一
　　The One 110

83　yì 义
　　Righteousness 112

84　yìxiàng 意象
　　Yixiang (Imagery) 113

85　yīnyáng 阴阳
　　Yin and Yang 114

86 yǐnxiù 隐秀
　　Latent Sentiment and Evident Beauty 115

87 yǒu dé zhě bì yǒu yán 有德者必有言
　　Virtuous People Are Sure to Produce Fine Writing. 117

88 yǒujiào-wúlèi 有教无类
　　Education for All Without Discrimination 118

89 yǒuwú 有无
　　You and *Wu* 120

90 yuánqǐ 缘起
　　Dependent Origination 121

91 zhīyīn 知音
　　Resonance and Empathy 122

92 zhíxún 直寻
　　Direct Quest 124

93 zhōngguó 中国
　　Zhongguo (China) 125

94 zhōnghuá 中华
　　Zhonghua 126

95 zhōngyōng 中庸
　　Zhongyong (Golden Mean) 128

96 zīwèi 滋味
　　Nuanced Flavor 129

97 zǐzhīduózhū 紫之夺朱
　　Purple Prevailing over Red 130

98 zìrán 自然
Naturalness 132

99 zìrán-yīngzhǐ 自然英旨
Charm of Spontaneity 133

100 zōngfǎ 宗法
Feudal Clan System 135

术语表 List of Concepts 137
中国历史年代简表 A Brief Chronology of Chinese History 143

bēikǎi 悲慨

Depressed and Enraged

悲伤愤慨。慨，感慨，愤慨。是晚唐诗人司空图（837—908）所概括的诗歌的二十四种风格之一。主要指诗作中所表现出的悲剧性情结。当诗人命途多舛或身处困境，或面对壮阔景观或大的事件而自觉力量渺小，会产生忧愁、悲哀、感伤、激愤的情绪，投射到诗歌创作中则形成"悲慨"风格。这一术语看似近于西方文学理论的"悲剧"范畴，实质上受道家思想影响较大，而最后往往或趋于无奈或趋于旷达。

Feeling depressed and enraged, which here refers to a sense of helplessness found in poems, is one of the 24 poetic styles summarized by Sikong Tu (837-908), a poet in the late Tang Dynasty. Faced with frustrations and tough challenges in life, or overwhelmed by the immensity of nature or major events, poets were often seized by dejection, grief, sadness, and anger, which gave rise to a "depressed and enraged" style in poetry writing. While the style bears similarity with the genre of tragedy in Western literary tradition, it is more influenced by Daoism, often featuring a sense of resignation or stoic optimism.

引例 Citations：

◎大风卷水，林木为摧。适苦欲死，招憩不来。百岁如流，富贵冷灰。大道日丧，若为雄才。壮士拂剑，浩然弥哀。萧萧落叶，漏雨苍苔。（司空图《二十四诗品·悲慨》）

（大风卷起狂澜，树木遭受摧折。心中悲苦痛不欲生，想休憩片刻亦不可得。百年岁月像流水永逝，富贵繁华都化作冷寂尘埃。大道日益不行，谁才是当世雄才？壮士拔剑仰天叹，凝望苍穹愈悲哀。好比落叶萧萧下，且听漏雨滴苍苔。）

Winds are howling, waves raging, and tree branches breaking. Gripped by an agonizing pain at my heart, I yearn for a spell of peace but only in vain. As time slips by, year after year, decade after decade, all the riches, fame, and splendor are but nothing. Facing moral degeneration, who will rise and salvage the world? With sword in hand, I heave a deep sigh and stare intensely at the sky. Overwhelmed with sorrow, all I can do is to watch leaves falling and hear rain beating against the moss. (Sikong Tu: Twenty-four Styles of Poetry)

◎感叹之余，作诗相属，托物悲慨，厄穷而不怨，泰而不骄。（苏轼《和王晋卿［并叙］》）
（在感叹之余，蒙其作诗劝慰嘱咐，借景物抒发内心悲伤愤慨的情绪，虽遇困厄而不怨恨，命运通达也不骄狂。）

After a deep sigh, he wrote a poem to admonish and comfort me, in which he expressed his indignation and resentment by making an analogy with imagery. He advised me not to grudge about tough times or be complacent when everything goes well in life. (Su Shi: A Poem in Reply to Wang Jinqing with a Preface)

běnmò 本末

Ben and Mo (The Fundamental and the Incidental)

本义指草木的根和梢，引申而为中国哲学的重要概念。其含义可以概括为三个方面：其一，指具有不同价值和重要性的事物，根本的、主要的事物为"本"，非根本的、次要的事物为"末"；其二，世界的本体或本原为"本"，具体的事物或现象为"末";其三,在道家的政治哲学中,无为之治下的自然状态为"本",各种具体的道德、纲常为"末"。在"本末"对待的关系中,"本"具有根本性、主导性的作用和意义,"末"由"本"而生,依赖"本"而存在,但"本"的作用的发挥仍需以"末"为载体。二者既相互区别,又相互依赖。

The two characters literally mean the different parts of a plant, namely, its root and its foliage. The extended meaning is an important concept in Chinese philosophical discourse. The term can be understood in three different ways. 1) *Ben* (本) refers to what is fundamental or essential, while *mo* (末) means what is minor or incidental, two qualities that differ in value and importance. 2) *Ben* refers to the existence of the world in an ontological sense, while *mo* represents any specific thing or phenomenon. 3) In Daoist political philosophy *ben* is a state in which rule is exercised by not disrupting the natural order of the world, while *mo* refers to moral standards and fundamental principles governing social behavior. In any *ben-mo* relationship, *ben* is most important and plays a dominant role, while *mo* exists thanks to *ben*. On the other hand, it is through the vehicle of *mo* that *ben* exerts its influence. Thus the two, though different, are mutually dependent.

引例 Citations:

◎子夏之门人小子,当洒扫应对进退,则可矣,抑末也。本之则无,如之何?(《论语·子张》)

(子夏的学生,叫他们做打扫、接待、应对的工作,那是可以的,不过这只是末节罢了。而那些最根本性的学问却没有学习,这怎么行呢?)

Zixia's students can clean, receive guests, and engage in social interaction, but these are trivial things. They have not learned the fundamentals. How can this be sufficient? (*The Analects*)

◎崇本以举其末。(王弼《老子注》)

(崇尚自然无为之本以统括道德礼法之末。)

One should respect, not interfere with, the natural order of the world, and apply this principle when establishing moral standards, social norms, and laws and regulations. (Wang Bi: *Annotations on Laozi*)

bōrě 般若

Prajna / Wisdom

梵文 prajñā 的音译(或译为"波若")。意为"智慧",指能洞见一切事物本性、认识万物真相的最高的智慧。佛教认为,"般若"是超越一切世俗认识的特殊智慧,是觉悟得道、修成佛或菩萨的所有修行方法的指南或根本。然而,这种智慧本身无形无相,不可言说,仅能依赖各种方便法门而有所领悟。

The term is the transliteration of the Sanskrit word *prajñā*, meaning wisdom. It refers to the supreme wisdom with insight into the nature and reality of all things. Buddhism believes that such wisdom surpasses all secular understandings, and therefore is the guide for or essence of the effort aimed at achieving enlightenment and attaining Buddhahood or bodhisattvahood. This wisdom has no form, no appearance, and cannot be expressed in words. It can only be achieved by undertaking a variety of accessible Buddhist practices.

引例 Citation：

◎般若无所知，无所见。(僧肇《肇论》引《道行般若经》)
(般若这种智慧不是普通的知识，也超越一切具体的见闻。)

Prajñā is the wisdom that surpasses all common or ordinary knowledge and specific understandings. (*The Perfection of Wisdom in Eight Thousand Lines and Its Verse Summary*, as cited in Seng Zhao: *Treatise of Seng Zhao*)

bù xué《shī》, wú yǐ yán 不学《诗》，无以言

You Won't Be Able to Talk Properly with Others Without Studying *The Book of Songs*.

不学习《诗经》，就不能提高与人交流和表达的能力。孔子（前551—前479）时代，《诗经》象征着一个人的社会身份与文化修养。不学习《诗经》，就无法参与君子间的各种交往，就不能提高语言表达能力。孔子对《诗经》与社会交往关系的论述，实际阐明了文学的教育功能或者说文学在教育中的重要地位。

In Confucius' (551-479 BC) time, how well one understood *The Book of Songs* was a sign of his social status and cultural attainment. If one did not study it, one would find it difficult to improve one's ability to express oneself and to converse with people of high social status. Confucius' elaboration on the relationship between studying *The Book of Songs* and social interaction actually expounds on the importance of literature in education.

引例 Citation：

◎尝独立，鲤过于庭。曰："学《诗》乎？"对曰："未也。""不学《诗》，无以言。"(《论语·季氏》)
(孔子曾独自站在堂上，儿子伯鱼从堂下庭院经过，孔子问他："学习《诗经》了吗？"伯鱼回答："没有。"孔子说："不学习《诗经》，就不会交流与表达。")

Confucius was standing alone in the central hall when his son Boyu walked across the front yard. Confucius asked, "Have you studied *The Book of Songs*?" "Not yet," was the reply. Confucius then said, "If you do not study it, you will not be able to express yourself properly." (*The Analects*)

chéng 诚

Sincerity

真实无妄。"诚"是儒家思想的核心概念之一，儒家认为，"诚"是"天道"或"天理"的本质，是万物得以存在的根据。同时，"诚"也是道德的本原和基础，一切道德的行为必须建立在内心真实无妄之上，否则便是虚妄，《中庸》称之为"不诚无物"。圣人以"诚"为本性，其言行自然与"天道""天理"相合；君子则以"诚"作为道德修养的目标以及达于"天道""天理"的途径。

Sincerity is among the core concepts of the Confucian school of thought. Basically, it means truthfulness without deceit. Confucians believed that sincerity is the essence of the "way of heaven" or "principles of heaven," a basis on which everything else is built. At the same time, sincerity is also the root and foundation of morality. All moral deeds must be conducted on the basis of sincerity from the bottom of the heart. Otherwise, they are nothing but pretensions. *The Doctrine of the Mean* maintains, "Nothing can be achieved without sincerity." Sages are sincere by nature. Therefore, their words and deeds are naturally consistent with the "way of heaven" and the "principles of heaven." *Junzi* (a man of virtue) upholds sincerity as his goal for moral attainment and an approach to achieving the "way of heaven" and the "principles of heaven."

引例 Citations：

◎诚者，天之道也；诚之者，人之道也。(《礼记·中庸》)

("诚"，是天的法则；达到"诚"，是人的修养路径。)

Being as it is is the way of nature; being true to human nature is the way to achieve self-refinement. (*The Book of Rites*)

◎诚者，真实无妄之谓，天理之本然也。(朱熹《中庸章句》)

("诚"就是真实不伪诈，是天理本来的状态。)

Sincerity means utter truthfulness without any pretensions or deceit. It is the natural state of the principles of heaven. (Zhu Xi: *Annotations on The Doctrine of the Mean*)

dàtóng 大同

Universal Harmony

儒家理想中的天下一家、人人平等、友爱互助的太平盛世（与"小康"相对）。儒家认为它是人类社会发展的最高阶段，类似于西方的乌托邦。其主要特征是：权力和财富归社会公有；社会平等，安居乐业；人人能得到社会的关爱；货尽其用，人尽其力。清末民初，"大同"又被用来指称西方传来的社会主义、共产主义、世界主义等概念。

This term refers to the time of peace and prosperity envisioned by Confucian scholars when all the people under heaven are one family, equal, friendly, and helpful to each other (as opposed to *xiaokang* [小康] – moderate prosperity). Confucianism takes universal harmony as the supreme stage of the development of the human society, somewhat similar to the idea of utopia in the West. Its main features are: All power and wealth belong to the whole of society; all people are equal and live and work in peace and contentment; everyone is cared for by society; everything is used to its fullest and everyone works to his maximum potential. In the late Qing Dynasty and the early Republic of China, the term referred to the concepts of socialism, communism, or cosmopolitanism that had been introduced to China from the West.

引例 Citation：

◎大道之行也，天下为（wéi）公。选贤与能，讲信修睦。故人不独亲其亲，不独子其子，使老有所终，壮有所用，幼有所长，矜寡孤独废疾者，皆有所养……是谓大同。(《礼记·礼运》)
（大道实行的时代，天下为天下人所共有。品德高尚、才能突出的人被选拔出来管理社会，人与人之间讲求诚实与和睦。所以人们不仅仅爱自己的双亲，不仅仅抚养自己的子女，而是使老年人都能终其天年，壮年人都有用武之地，幼童都能得到抚育，无妻或丧妻的年老男子、无夫或丧夫的年老女子、丧父的儿童、无子女的老人以及残障者都能得到照顾和供养……这就叫做大同社会。）

When the Great Way prevails, the world belongs to all the people. People of virtue and competence are chosen to govern the country; honesty is valued and people live in harmony. People not only love their parents, bring up their children, but also take care of the aged. The middle-aged are able to put their talents and abilities to best use, children are well nurtured, and old widows and widowers, unmarried old people, orphans, childless old people, and the disabled are all provided for… This is universal harmony. (*The Book of Rites*)

dào 道

Dao (Way)

本义指人所行之路，引申而有三重含义：其一，指不同领域的事物所遵循的法则，如日月星辰运行的规律称为天道，人事活动所遵循的规律称为人道；其二，指万事万物所遵循的普遍法则；其三，指事物的本原或本体，超越于有形的具体事物，是万物生成的基始，又是万物存在和人类行为的根据。儒家、道家、佛教等都谈论道，其内涵差异甚大。儒家之道以仁义礼乐为基本内容，佛教和道家之道偏重"空""无"方面的意义。

In its original meaning, *dao* (道) is the way or path taken by people. It has three extended meanings: 1) the general laws followed by things in different spheres, e.g. the natural order by which the sun, moon and stars move is called the way of heaven; the rules that govern human activities are the way of man; 2) the universal patterns followed by all things and beings; and 3) the original source or ontological existence of things, which transcends form and constitutes the basis for the birth and existence of all things, and for the activities of human beings. In their respective discussions of Dao, Confucianism, Daoism, and Buddhism imbue it with very different connotations. While benevolence, righteousness, social norms, and music education form the basic content of the Confucian Dao, the Buddhist and Daoist Dao tends to emphasize *kong* (空 emptiness) and *wu* (无 void).

引例 Citations：

◎天道远，人道迩。(《左传·昭公十八年》)

（天之道遥远，人事之道切近。）

The way of heaven is far away; the way of man is near. (*Zuo's Commentary on The Spring and Autumn Annals*)

◎形而上者谓之道。(《周易·系辞上》)

（未成形质者称为道。）

What is above form is called Dao. (*The Book of Changes*)

dé 德

De (Virtue)

　　"德"有两种不同含义：其一，指个人的良好品格或人们在社会共同生活中的良好品行。"德"原初的意义与行为有关，主要指外在的道德行为，后兼指与道德行为相应的内在的情感、意识，"德"被认为是外在的道德行为与内在的道德情感、道德意识的结合。其二，指事物从"道"所得的特殊规律或特性，是幽隐无形的"道"的具体显现，也是事物产生和存在的内在依据。

The term has two different meanings. One is an individual's fine moral character, or his proper conduct in society. At first *de* (德) was only related to an individual's behavior, referring to his external moral conduct. Later, it also referred to something that combined external behavior with internal emotions and moral consciousness. The other meaning of *de* refers to the special laws and features obtained from Dao, or the physical manifestation of the hidden and formless Dao, as well as the internal basis for the origination and existence of all things.

引例 Citations：

◎天生烝民，有物有则，民之秉彝，好是懿德。(《诗经·大雅·烝民》)
(上天降生众民，有事物就有法则，民众遵守普遍的法则，崇好这样的美德。)

Heaven gives birth to people, provides them with goods and materials, and subjects them to rules. People obey universal rules and value virtues. (*The Book of Songs*)

◎道生之，德畜之。(《老子·五十一章》)
(道生成万物，德蓄养万物。)

Dao creates all things under heaven while *de* nurtures them. (*Laozi*)

fāfèn-zhùshū 发愤著书

Indignation Spurs One to Write Great Works.

因在现实生活中遭遇不平而下决心写出传世著作。源出《史记·太史公自序》。西汉司马迁（前145或前135？—？）在遭受宫刑后，强烈的愤懑情绪成为他创作《史记》的驱动力。他借《史记》表达自己的思想、感情、志向，最终使著作流传于世。"发愤著书"后多用来解释优秀的文艺作品的创作动机和原因。这一术语揭示了优秀的文学作品的产生往往与作者个人的不幸遭遇有直接关联。后世在此基础上又衍生出"不平则鸣""诗穷而后工"等观点。

This term means suffering injustice in life can spur one to create great works. It originated from the "Preface by the Grand Historian to *Records of the Historian*." After Sima Qian (145 or 135?-? BC), an official in the Western Han Dynasty, suffered the unjust punishment of castration, his indignation spurred him to write the great work, *Records of the Historian*. In the book he gave expression to his thoughts, feelings, and aspirations, which made the book a classic for later generations. The expression "indignation spurs one to write great works" was used to explain one of the motivations and reasons for creating masterpieces. It points to the fact that injustice suffered by an author often turns out to be the source of inspiration for him to write a literary masterpiece. It later led to similar terms like "cry out against injustice" and "a good poem is the product of pent-up emotions."

引例 Citations:

◎惜诵以致愍兮,发愤以抒情。(屈原《九章·惜诵》)
(痛惜直言进谏却招致谗毁疏远,怀着一腔忧愤抒发衷情。)

I am saddened that my frank remonstration with the king has brought false accusations on me and left me in exile. In anguish and indignation, I am writing these poems to express my strong feelings. (Qu Yuan: *Collection of Nine Pieces*)

◎《诗》三百篇,大抵贤圣发愤之所为作也。此人皆意有所郁结,不得通其道,故述往事、思来者。(《史记·太史公自序》)
(《诗经》三百篇,大都是圣贤抒发忧愤而创作出来的。这些人都是感情郁结,不能实现志向,所以记述往事,希望将来的人能够了解。)

Most of the 300 poems in *The Book of Songs* were written by sages who were in anguish and indignation. They were depressed over what had prevented them from fulfilling their aspirations, so they composed poems about what had happened in the hope that future generations would understand them. (*Records of the Historian*)

fǎzhì 法治

Rule by Law

以法治国。是站在君主的角度，主张君主通过制定并严格执行法令、规章来治理民众和国家（与"人治"相对），是先秦时期法家的重要政治思想。法家的"法治"思想有赏罚分明的一面，也有过于严苛、刚硬的弊端。自汉朝以迄清朝，"法治"和"人治"，各王朝多兼而用之。近代以降，"法治"因西学东渐而被赋予新的含义。

Rule by law, as opposed to rule by man, calls for ruling a state and its people by the ruler through enacting and strictly enforcing laws and regulations. It is an important political thought of the Legalist scholars in the pre-Qin period. Rule by law meted out well-defined rewards and punishments, but tended to be excessively severe and rigid in enforcement. From the Han Dynasty all the way to the Qing Dynasty, rule by law and rule by man were exercised by various dynasties, mostly in combination. With the spread of Western thoughts to China in more recent times, rule by law acquired new meanings.

引例 Citations：

◎是故先王之治国也，不淫意于法之外，不为惠于法之内也。(《管子·明

法》)

(所以先王治国,不在法度外恣意妄为,也不在法度内私行恩惠。)

When our forefathers ruled the state, they did not act unscrupulously in disregard of law, nor did they bestow personal favors within the framework of law. (*Guanzi*)

◎ 故法治者,治之极轨也,而通五洲万国数千年间。其最初发明此法治主义,以成一家言者谁乎?则我国之管子也!(梁启超《管子传》第六章)

(所以法治就是治理国家的最高模式,它通行于五大洲万国的数千年历史之中。那么最初发明法治主义,成为一家之言的人是谁呢?是我国的管子啊!)

Therefore, rule by law is the supreme way to rule a country. It has been exercised by numerous countries in the world for several thousand years. Who conceived this idea and developed it into a theory of governance? It was none other than our fellow countryman Guanzi! (Liang Qichao: *A Biography of Guanzi*)

fēng-yǎ-sòng 风雅颂

Ballad, Court Hymn, and Eulogy

《诗经》中依体裁与音乐对诗歌所分出的类型。"风(国风)"是不同地区的音乐,大部分是民歌;"雅"是宫廷宴享或朝会时的乐歌,分为"大雅"与"小雅",大部分是贵族文人的作品;"颂"是宗庙祭祀用的舞曲歌辞,内容多是歌颂祖先的功业。"雅""颂"指雅正之音,而"国风"系民间乐歌,因此"风雅颂"既是《诗经》的体裁,同时也有高雅纯正的含义。"风雅"后来一般指典雅与高雅的事物。

In *The Book of Songs,* the content is divided into three categories according to style and tune: *feng* (ballad), *ya* (court hymn), and *song* (eulogy). Ballads are music from different regions, mostly folk songs. Court hymns, divided into *daya* (major hymn) and *xiaoya* (minor hymn), are songs sung at court banquets or grand ceremonies. They are mostly the works by lettered noblemen. Eulogies are ritual or sacrificial dance music and songs, most of which praise the achievements of ancestors. Court hymns and eulogies are highbrow songs while ballads are lowbrow ones. Therefore, ballads, court hymns, and eulogies not only refer to the styles of *The Book of Songs* but also classify the songs into highbrow and lowbrow categories. Later on *fengya* (风雅) generally referred to anything elegant.

引例 Citations：

◎故《诗》有六义焉：一曰风，二曰赋，三曰比，四曰兴，五曰雅，六曰颂。(《毛诗序》)

（所以《诗经》有六项基本内容：即风、赋、比、兴、雅、颂。）

Therefore *The Book of Songs* has six basic elements: ballads, narratives, analogies, associations, court hymns, and eulogies. (Introductions to *Mao's Version of The Book of Songs*)

◎"三经"是赋、比、兴，是做诗底骨子，无诗不有，才无则不成诗。盖不是赋便是比，不是比便是兴。如风、雅、颂却是里面横弗（chǎn）底，都有赋、比、兴，故谓之"三纬"。(《朱子语类》卷八十)

(《诗经》中的"三经"指赋、比、兴，是作诗的骨架，所有的诗都有，如果没有就不成诗。大概是没有赋就得有比，没有比就得有兴。像风、雅、颂在诗歌里面却起横向的贯穿作用，诗歌中都得有赋、比、兴，所以将风、雅、颂称为"三纬"。)

The three "longitudes" of *The Book of Songs* refer to narrative, analogy, and association, which serve as the frame of a poem. Without these, they could not be called poems. If narrative is not used in a poem, analogy must be used; if analogy is not used, association must be employed. Ballads from the states, court hymns, and eulogies play a connecting role in the poems. Since the poems have narrative, analogy, and association serving as the "longitudes," ballads from the states, court hymns, and eulogies are therefore called the three "latitudes." (*Classified Conversations of Master Zhu Xi*)

fēngjiàn 封建

Feudal System / Feudalism

即封邦建国。古代帝王将爵位、土地和人口分封给亲戚和功臣，让他们在封地内建国。各封国规模小于王室直辖领地；在遵循王室统治秩序的前提下，各封国在军、政等方面具有很高的自主性；封国之间相互制衡，共同拱卫王室。封国的世袭要经王室确认，并按规定向王室缴纳贡赋。作为一种政治制度，封建制相传始于黄帝时期，至西周时期达于完备；它与基于血缘家族制而形成的宗法制互为表里，并随之衍生出等级身份制等。秦始皇（前259—前210）统一中国后，废除封建制，实行郡县制。自此直到清代，在中国占主导地位的是中央集权制或专制帝制；而"封建"作为专制帝制下的一种辅助性手段，或隐或显地存在着。

In feudalism, the lord granted titles of nobility, fiefs, and people to his relatives and officials and allowed them to establish dukedoms. A fief was smaller than the territory under the direct control of the lord. While obeying the rule of the lord, a dukedom enjoyed a high degree of autonomy in its military and administrative affairs. Dukedoms checked each other in the protection of the lord. A dukedom might be passed down genetically upon the approval of the lord and was required to pay tribute to him. As a political system, feudalism is believed to have started in the era of the legendary Yellow Emperor, and became established in the Western Zhou Dynasty. Feudalism was akin to the patriarchal clan system based on blood ties and gave rise to a hierarchy system. After the First Emperor of Qin (259-210 BC) reunified China, he abolished feudalism in favor of the system of prefectures and counties. From the Qin Dynasty to the Qing Dynasty, centralized government or imperial autocracy was dominant in China, rendering feudalism, which existed overtly or covertly, supplementary.

引例 Citation：

◎彼封建者，更古圣王尧、舜、禹、汤、文、武而莫能去之。（柳宗元《封建论》）

（封建制经历了上古的圣贤之王尧、舜、禹、商汤、周文王、周武王也没有能废除它。）

Feudal system survived the eras of all ancient sages, namely Yao, Shun, Yu the Great, Tang of Shang, King Wen of Zhou, and King Wu of Zhou. (Liu Zongyuan: On Feudal System)

fěngyù 讽谕

Subtle Admonition

指文学作品借用一定事例或思想，含蓄婉转地向统治者传达民情民风、批评时政，从而使统治者能够接受讽谏，革除弊政。"讽"是指讽谏、劝诫，要求诗文中的批评语言含蓄婉转；"谕"是晓谕、表明，文章主旨最终要归结为劝鉴、批评。也就是说，它实际包含密不可分的两方面：一是文学的表达方式（"讽"要婉转含蓄），二是文学的社会功能（"晓谕"统治者）。"讽谕说"由汉代学者解释《诗经》时总结提出，儒家以此倡导文学对朝廷教化和社会民风的干预作用，将其视为文学的特殊使命。唐代诗人白居易（772—846）大量创作讽谕诗，强化诗歌创作的社会功能，推进了这一文学传统，对后世文学创作影响很大。

The term refers to the use of allegories to convey popular mood and public opinion and make critical comments on state affairs to the ruler in a tactful manner in the hope to persuade him to correct wrong policies. *Feng* (讽) represents making critical but persuasive comments subtly through poetry or prose; *yu* (喻) means delivering an explicit message. Such literary writing is intended to be both critical and persuasive; and it has two integral aspects, namely, a subtle literary way of expression as required by *feng*, and its social function of sending explicit messages to the ruler as required. The theory of subtle admonition was advocated by scholars of the Han Dynasty based on their interpretation of *The Book of Songs*. Confucian scholars from then on promoted the use of subtle admonition to influence decision-making of the ruler and social mores in a literary way. Bai Juyi (772-846), a poet of the Tang Dynasty, wrote many such poems, further reinforcing the social function of poetry and advancing this literary tradition, which had great impact on literary creation of later generations.

引例 **Citations**：

◎或以抒下情而通讽谕，或以宣上德而尽忠孝。（班固《两都赋序》）
（有些作品表达臣民的思想感情同时也希望由此将其中的讽喻传达给君王，

有些作品则是宣扬君主的恩德同时引导臣民克尽忠孝义务。）

Some literary works use subtle admonition to convey what the subjects think and feel, in the hope that the subtle advice could reach the ruler, whereas other works expound the kindness and benevolence of the ruler so as to guide the populace to fulfilling their duties and obligations. (Ban Gu: Preface to "Essays on Chang'an and Luoyang")

◎古之为文者，上以纫王教，系国风；下以存炯戒，通讽谕。（白居易《策林·六八·议文章》）

（古人写文章，往大了说是为了阐明朝廷教化与社会民风的关联，往小了说是保存谏戒、传达讽喻。）

Writings by ancient scholars could be said that at a higher level they aimed at explaining some kind of link between the ideas of the ruling court and popular sentiment in society. At a more practical level, they sent a clear message of advice to the rulers through allegories. (Bai Juyi: *Collection of Essays in Preparation for the Final Round of the Imperial Examination*)

fù-bǐ-xìng 赋比兴

Narrative, Analogy, and Association

《诗经》创作的三种表现手法。"赋"是铺陈事物直接叙述；"比"是类比；"兴"是先言他物以引出所咏之词，有两层含义，一是即兴感发，二是在感发时借客观景物婉转地表达出某种思想感情。"赋比兴"为汉代儒家所总结和提出，后来演变为中国古代文学创作的基本原则和方法。

These are the three ways of expression employed in *The Book of Songs*:

a narrative is a direct reference to an object or an event, an analogy metaphorically likens one thing to another, and an association is an impromptu expression of a feeling, a mood or a thought, or using an objective thing as metaphor for sensibilities. Confucian scholars of the Han Dynasty summarized and formulated this concept of narrative, analogy, and association, which later became the basic principle and method in classical Chinese literary creation.

引例 Citation：

◎赋、比、兴是《诗》之所用，风、雅、颂是《诗》之成形。(《毛诗序》孔颖达正义)

(赋、比、兴是《诗经》创作的三种手法，风、雅、颂是《诗经》体制上的定型。)

In *The Book of Songs,* narrative, analogy, and association are three techniques in its creation, whereas ballad, court hymn, and eulogy represent three established styles of the poems. (Kong Yingda: Correct Meaning of "Introductions to *Mao's Version of The Book of Songs*")

gédiào 格调

Form and Melody

指诗歌的体制声调，包括思想旨趣和声律形式两方面，涉及诗歌批评的品味与境界。"格"指诗歌的体制合乎规范，"调"指诗歌的声调韵律。唐宋时期的一些诗论家倡导格调，意在确立诗歌的雅正标准。明清以后的格调说，多强调作品应符合儒家正统思想，这影响了诗人的情感表达与艺术创作。"格调"后来也用到其他文艺领域。

The term refers to the form and metrical patterns, as well as content, of poetry. It relates to artistic taste and appeal in poetry criticism. *Ge* (格) refers to the need to satisfy established metrical rules, while *diao* (调) refers to the need to follow tone and rhyme schemes in poetry. Some poetry critics of the Tang and Song dynasties stressed the importance of form and melody in order to establish a set of elegant and authoritative standards for poetry. Theory on form and melody in the Ming and Qing dynasties often emphasized the importance for poets to abide by Confucian orthodoxy, thus constraining their expression of feelings and artistic creations. The term was later also used in discussions of other forms of art.

引例 Citations：

◎高古者格，宛亮者调。（李梦阳《驳何氏论文书》）
（高雅古朴就是"格"，婉曲清亮就是"调"。）

To be elegant and unaffected is to satisfy the requirements of form; to be tuneful and resonant is to follow the rules of melody. (Li Mengyang: *Arguments Against He Jingming's Views*)

◎白石词以清虚为体，而时有阴冷处，格调最高。（陈廷焯《白雨斋词话》卷二）
（姜夔的词以清新虚空为主要特色，虽然有时有凄清冷寂的地方，但格调最高。）

Jiang Kui's poems are characterized by ethereal purity. Though tinged with loneliness and sadness at times, they are of high standard and taste. (Chen Tingzhuo: *Remarks on Ci Poetry from White Rain Studio*)

huáxià 华夏

Huaxia / The Han People

古代居住于中原地区的汉民族先民的自称。最早称"华""诸华"或"夏""诸夏"。"华夏"实际表达的是以汉民族为主体的中原先民对其共同的生活、语言、文化特征的一种认同和传承。秦建立以华夏为主体的统一的多民族国家以后，华夏才成为比较稳定的族群。自汉代以后，华夏又有了"汉"这一名称与之并用。后来华夏进一步引申为指中国或汉族。

The forefathers of the Han people living in the Central Plains referred to themselves by this term. Earlier on they called themselves Hua (华), Zhuhua (诸华), Xia (夏) or Zhuxia (诸夏). The term Huaxia (华夏) embodies the common identity of the way of life, language, and culture of the people living in the Central Plains, mainly the Han people, and the inheritance of such identity. The Huaxia people evolved into a fairly stable ethnic group in the Qin Dynasty, which established a unified country of many ethnic groups with Huaxia being the principal group. In the Han Dynasty, the term Han became an alternative name of Huaxia. Later, the term Huaxia was extended to refer to China or the Han people.

引例 Citation：

◎夏，大也。中国有礼义之大，故称夏；有服章之美，谓之华。华夏一也。（《左传·定公十年》孔颖达正义）

（夏的含义是"大"。华夏族的礼仪宏富伟大，所以称为"夏"；华夏族的衣服华美出众，所以称为"华"。"华"与"夏"是同一个意思。）

The Chinese character 夏 (*xia*) means big and great. Since the ancient Huaxia people practiced grand and elaborate rituals, they called themselves Xia (great). Their dresses were resplendent, so they were referred to as *Hua* (splendid). Therefore, both *Hua* and *Xia* refer to the Han people. (Kong Yingda: *Correct Meaning of Zuo's Commentary on The Spring and Autumn Annals*)

huáiyuǎn-yǐdé 怀远以德

Embrace Distant Peoples by Means of Virtue

指用恩惠、仁德去安抚、怀柔边远地区的部族、民众等。是历代华夏族政权用以处理与其他民族、未纳入直接统治范围的边远部族以及外国关系的一种政治理念，也是"以德服人"思想的重要方面。中国是一个多民族国家，以华夏族为主体的政权，自认为是大国并且文化发达，对于那些远离中华文化的边远部族、民众等，一般不采取武力征服，而是用比较温和、合于儒家"仁德"的手段，达到安抚并使之归顺的目的。

This expression refers to pursuing conciliatory and benevolent policies and offering benefits to tribes and groups in remote areas. It was a political concept adopted by successive governments led mostly by the Han people in their relations with other ethnic groups, tribes in remote areas not yet directly under their rule, and foreign states. It also represented an important component of the theory of winning over others by virtue. China was, as it is today, a multi-ethnic country. The Han-led government ruled over a large territory and believed that they had an advanced culture. They usually took a conciliatory approach based on the Confucian concept of benevolence in dealing with the tribes and populations in remote regions, rather than conquering them by force, with the goal of placating them and winning their allegiance.

引例 Citation：

◎管仲言于齐侯曰：臣闻之，招携以礼，怀远以德，德礼不易，无人不怀。（《左传·僖公七年》）

（管仲对齐侯道：臣听说，招抚尚未归顺的诸侯，用礼；安抚边远地区的部族、民众，用德。不违背德和礼，没有人会不归附。）

Guan Zhong said to the Marquis of Qi, "I have heard it said: Win over the disaffected with respect and embrace distant peoples with virtue. With virtue and respect unchanging, there is no one that will not be embraced." (*Zuo's Commentary on The Spring and Autumn Annals*)

肌理

Reasoning and Structure

本义指肌肉的纹理，引申指事物细密的条理。作为文学术语由清代翁方纲（1733—1818）首先提出，兼指义理与文理两方面：义理是诗歌所阐述的道理或事理，主要指合乎儒家的思想和学问；文理是诗歌的条理或脉理，主要指诗歌的结构、格律和各种创作技法。明清以来，性灵派倡导文学抒发个体性情，摒弃教化；神韵派赞美诗歌意境的空灵玄虚。翁方纲反对这两种诗学主张，推崇宋诗的创作原则与方法，强调诗歌在义理上以经义为准绳，以学问为根底；文理上强调精细缜密，形式雅丽、穷形极变但要内容充实。清代乾嘉时期经学和考据之学盛行，肌理派就是在此背景下形成的诗派。翁方纲宣扬诗歌内容和形式的有机联系，推动了学人诗派的发展，但他一味鼓吹以学问考证作诗，受到同时代及后代文艺批评家的批评。

The term originally refers to the texture of muscle, and later by extension it refers to well-organized principles in things. As a literary term, it was first used by Weng Fanggang (1733-1818), a Qing-dynasty scholar, to refer to two aspects: *yili* (义理 reasoning) and *wenli* (文理 structure). The former is about views or reasoning, primarily concerning Confucian thinking and learning expressed in poetry; whereas the latter represents texture of poetry, especially poetic structures, metrical schemes and rhythms, and other techniques of writing. Scholars of the Xingling School (School of Inner Self) of the Ming and Qing dynasties advocated rejecting dogmatic guidelines and expressing one's emotions and thoughts in literary works, while adherents of the Shenyun School (School of Elegant Subtlety) believed in ethereal beauty and implicitness expressed through poetry. Criticizing both literary trends, Weng promoted the principles and techniques of the Song-dynasty poetry. In terms of *yili*, he emphasized the need to follow classical Confucian tradition and erudition. In terms of *wenli*, he advocated exquisite intricacy, attention to details, and graceful structures with a great many variations, as well as the need to convey a substantive message. During the reign of Emperor Qianlong (1736-1795) and Emperor Jiaqing (1796-1820) of the Qing Dynasty, a boom in the study of Confucian classics and textual research led to the emergence of the Jili School (School of Reasoning and Structure). Weng advocated integration of form and content in poetry, thus promoting the development of poetry based on classic learning. However, his overemphasis on classic scholarliness in poetry was criticized by scholars of both his age and later generations.

引例 Citations：

◎同之与异，不屑古今，擘肌分理，唯务折衷。（刘勰《文心雕龙·序志》）

（我不介意自己的见解与前人的见解是否相同，也不介意这些见解来自古人还是今人，只是通过对文章的条理和义理进行细致剖分，力求找到不偏不倚、最为合理的看法。）

I don't care if my views differ from those of others, nor do I care if the differing views are from ancient scholars or my contemporaries. What I do care is analyzing carefully the structure and reasoning of writings in order to arrive at a balanced view. (Liu Xie: *The Literary Mind and the Carving of Dragons*)

◎义理之理，即文理之理，即肌理之理也。（翁方纲《〈志言集〉序》）

（诠释儒家经典所追寻的"义理"中的"理"，实质上就是文章的道理和事理，也是文章的脉理和条理。）

Yili in Confucian classics is all about structure and reasoning in writing, i.e., the texture and proper presentation of writings. (Weng Fanggang: Preface to *Collection of Weng's Poems*)

◎士生今日，经籍之光盈溢于世宙，为学必以考证为准，为诗必以肌理为准。（翁方纲《〈志言集〉序》）

（士人生于这个年代，正值儒学繁荣昌盛，辉映世间，因此，做学问的人必以查考验证为标准，写诗的人必以遵循肌理为标准。）

Today's men of letters are in an era when Confucian studies are flourishing. It is therefore imperative that scholars base their study on research and verification, and that poets focus on the structure and reasoning of their works. (Weng Fanggang: Preface to *Collection of Weng's Poems*)

jiāngshān 江山

Rivers and Mountains / Country or State Power

本义指河流和山岭，代指一个国家的政权及其所覆盖的全部疆域（义同"河山"）。这种用法隐含着这样的观念：河流、山岭地形险要，是卫护国家安全、政权稳固的天然屏障；疆域是国家的构成要素。

The term, similar in meaning to *heshan* (河山), literally means rivers and mountains. It is used to refer to the sovereignty of a state and all its territory. The term has these implications: rivers and mountains provide natural barriers that protect the country and its sovereignty; territory is the key feature of a state.

引例 Citation：

◎ 割据江山，拓土万里。(《三国志·吴书·贺邵传》)
（以武力占据一方，建立政权，开拓大片疆土。）

To seize a region by force, establish a regime there, and extend its territory far and wide. (*The History of the Three Kingdoms*)

jiàohuà 教化

Shaping the Mind Through Education

指教育和感化。是中国古代重要的政治理念和治国方法。当政者一般通过行政命令、道德教育、环境影响、通俗读物传播、科举考试等诸种有形和无形的手段的综合运用，将主流价值观潜移默化地向民众普及，使之深入民众的日常活动之中，从而实现政治与风俗的合二为一。

Shaping the mind through education was a key concept of the political philosophy and an essential way of governance in ancient China. Rulers usually used a combination of means, both visible and invisible, to subtly spread their values among people so that these values would be observed in people's daily life, leading to integration of governance and social mores. These means include issuing administrative decrees, conducting moral education, creating a favorable environment, disseminating popular literature that promoted ethical values, and selecting officials through imperial examinations.

引例 Citation：

◎故礼之教化也微，其止邪也于未形。(《礼记·经解》)
（所以礼对民众的教育和感化作用是隐微的，它能够将不好的东西消弭于未成形之时。）

Educating and influencing the people through *li* (礼) has the invisible impact of getting rid of immoral thoughts in the bud. (*The Book of Rites*)

jiǔzhōu 九州

Nine *Zhou* (Regions)

中国的别称。《尚书·禹贡》中将中国划分为九州，分别是冀州、兖州、青州、徐州、扬州、荆州、豫州、梁州、雍州。同时代或稍后的典籍《周礼》《尔雅》《吕氏春秋》等有关"九州"的说法大同小异。"九州"作为行政区划在历史上并未真正实行过，但它反映了春秋末期以来中华先民栖息生活的大致上的地理范围。

This term is an alternative designation for China. According to *The Book of History*, the country consisted of nine *zhou* (州), namely Jizhou, Yanzhou, Qingzhou, Xuzhou, Yangzhou, Jingzhou, Yuzhou, Liangzhou, and Yongzhou. There are similar references to the nine *zhou* in classic works of the same or later period, such as *The Rites of Zhou*, *Er Ya*, and *Master Lü's Spring and Autumn Annals*. The nine *zhou* were never adopted as actual administrative divisions of the country, but they did show the general geographical area inhabited by the Chinese people since the late Spring and Autumn Period.

引例 Citations：

◎九州生气恃风雷，万马齐喑究可哀。我劝天公重抖擞，不拘一格降人才。（龚自珍《己亥杂诗》其一百二十五）
（九州生机勃勃靠的是风雷激荡，万马齐喑的局面实在令人悲哀。我奉劝上苍定要重振精神，打破一切清规戒律降生更多人才。）

The vitality of China depends on wind and thunder, unfortunately not a single horse's neighing is heard. I urge the Lord of Heaven to once again lift his spirits and, breaking all bonds and fetters, send talent of all kinds to the human world. (Gong Zizhen: *Miscellaneous Poems Written in the Year of 1839*)

◎吾恐中国之祸，不在四海之外，而在九州之内矣。（张之洞《劝学篇·序》）
（我恐怕中国的祸患，不在中国之外，而在中国之内。）

As I see it, the cause of China's disasters lies not overseas but within the country. (Zhang Zhidong: *Exhortation to Study*)

kējǔ 科举

The Imperial Civil Examination System

通过分科考试选用官吏的制度。隋文帝（541—604）统一中国后，废除以门第、品级为主的选人制度。隋炀帝（569—618）大业元年（公元605年）正式开科取士。历代科举，在考试科目、内容、录取规则上均有变化。各科之中，以进士科最难，也最为士人所重。元明以后，考试内容以《四书》《五经》文句命题，答题是写一篇文章，格式为八股文，观点需以《四书章句集注》等为依据。1905年光绪皇帝（1871—1908）下诏废科举。科举制促进了贵族政治向官僚政治的转换，同时兼具教育、选官、考试、社会分层、文化传承等多种功能。它是隋朝以后1300年间中国最主要的"选举"方式，对中国社会发生的影响是极其深广的。

This is the system in which officials were selected through different levels of examinations. After Emperor Wen of the Sui Dynasty (541-604) reunified China in 581, he abolished the system of selecting officials on the basis of family background or moral character. In 605, the first year of the reign of Emperor Yang of the Sui Dynasty (569-618), the system to select officials through imperial civil examinations was officially established. From then on, examination subjects, content, and recruitment standards varied from dynasty to dynasty. The *jinshi*, the highest level and the most difficult of imperial civil examinations, was always the most revered by scholars. In the Yuan and Ming dynasties, examination content was based on the Four Books and the Five Classics and had to be answered in the form of the "eight-legged" essay and refer to *Commentaries on the Four Books* and other classics. In 1905 Emperor Guangxu of the Qing Dynasty (1871-1908) issued an edict abolishing the imperial civil examination system.

For 1,300 years since the Sui Dynasty, the imperial civil examination system was the main method for selecting officials, which had a broad and profound influence on Chinese society. It hastened the transformation of aristocracy-based politics to bureaucracy-based politics and had multiple functions such as educating people, selecting officials, choosing talent through examinations, social stratification, and carrying forward the traditional culture.

引例 Citations：

◎［宋］太宗即位，思振淹滞，谓侍臣曰："朕欲博求俊彦于科场中，非敢望拔十得五，止得一二，亦可为致治之具矣。"（《宋史·选举志一》）
（宋太宗即位后，打算给那些有德有才却久遭埋没的人提供机会，对身边的大臣说："我想通过科举考试广求德才出众的人，并不指望选上十个人就有五个人出众，只要其中有一两个出众的，就可以把科举考试作为实现政治清平的手段了。"）

Soon after Emperor Taizong of the Song Dynasty ascended the throne, he wanted to help people with both moral integrity and professional competence come to prominence, so he said to his ministers, "By recruiting remarkable people through the imperial civil examination system, I do not expect five out of ten of those recruited to excel. If one or two out of ten do, the imperial civil examination system can be used as an effective means to maintain political stability." (*The History of the Song Dynasty*)

◎科举必由学校，而学校起家，可不由科举。（《明史·选举志一》）
（科举必须经由学校，但从学校推举上来的人才，可以不经过科举考试。）

The imperial civil examination system had to be implemented through schools, but those recommended by schools to official positions do not necessarily need to take the imperial civil examinations. (*The History of the Ming Dynasty*)

lài yǔ Xīshī, dào tōng wéi yī 厉与西施，道通为一

A Scabby Person and the Beautiful Lady Xishi Are the Same in the Eyes of Dao.

身长癞疮的人与美丽的西施，从道的角度看都可相通为一。厉，通"癞"，指长有癞疮的人。这是庄子（前369？—前286）关于审美相对性的著名论述。原意指身长癞疮的人与著名的美女没有区别，因为她们都是"道"的产物及体现。美丑的判断只是人们主观上的感觉而已，而且美丑之间还可相互转化。庄子的这一思想，强调从造物的本原看，美丑都符合道，都具有内在的同一性。这个思想启发后世的文艺评论家从相反相成的维度去看待自然万物与文学创作。

This is a famous statement made by Zhuangzi (369?-286 BC) on how beauty is relative. Originally it meant there was no difference between a beauty and an ugly person, because they both came from and reflected Dao. The character 厉 (*lai*) meant 癞 (*lai*, covered in scabs) in ancient Chinese. Whether a person is beautiful or ugly is but a subjective perspective in the mind of the beholder. Besides, beauty can turn into ugliness, and vice versa. Zhuangzi, from the perspective of the origin of all things, stressed that beauty and ugliness are both in accord with Dao and are inherently the same. This idea has encouraged later literary critics to look at all things, including literary works, from the perspective that opposite things complement each other.

引例 Citations：

◎举莛与楹，厉与西施，恢恑（guǐ）憰（jué）怪，道通为一。(《庄子·齐物论》)

（细小的草茎与高大的庭柱，身长癞疮的人与美丽的西施，还有各种诡变怪异的事物，从道的角度来说都可相通为一。）

In the light of Dao, a small blade of grass or a tall pillar, someone as ugly as a favus patient or someone as beautiful as Lady Xishi, as well as crafty and strange things, are all the same. (*Zhuangzi*)

◎大用外腓（féi），真体内充。返虚入魂，积健为雄。(司空图《二十四诗品·雄浑》)

（大道呈现于外显得雄浑阔大，真实的本体则充满于内。唯有返回虚静，内心才能到达浑然之境；积蓄精神力量，笔力才能雄放豪健。）

The grand appearance is an external manifestation of Dao, while the true vitality permeates itself internally. Reverting to a tranquil void, one may gain fullness and amass inner strength, and he will produce powerful works. (Sikong Tu: *Twenty-four Styles of Poetry*)

lè ér bù yín, āi ér bù shāng 乐而不淫，哀而不伤

Express Enjoyment Without Indulgence and Express Grief Without Excessive Distress

快乐而不放纵，悲哀而不伤身。原是孔子（前551—前479）对于《诗经·周南·关雎》中有关青年男女爱情描写的评语，后世儒家将其作为倡导

诗歌及其他文学作品中正平和、情理谐和之美的基本规范与评价标准。这一术语与儒家提倡的中庸思想相一致。近现代以来，其思想内涵也因受到时代潮流冲击而不断更新。

This is what Confucius (551-479 BC) said of the description of love between young men and women in the poem entitled "Guan Ju" in "Ballads of Zhounan," *The Book of Songs*. Later Confucian scholars regarded this as a basic requirement for poems and other literary works to advocate impartiality, peace of mind, and harmony between emotion and reason, making it a criterion for evaluating literary works. Its connotation is in accord with *zhongyong* (the golden mean) of Confucianism. In the more recent history, the connotation of the term has been continuously renewed to keep pace with the times.

引例 Citations：

◎《关雎》乐而不淫，哀而不伤。(《论语·八佾》)
(《关雎》快乐而不放纵，悲哀而不伤身。)

The poem "Guan Ju" expresses enjoyment without indulgence and grief without excessive distress. (*The Analects*)

◎《国风》好色而不淫，《小雅》怨诽而不乱。(《史记·屈原贾生列传》)
(《国风》虽然描写爱恋情欲，但是并不放纵；《小雅》虽有怨恨与批评，但是并不煽动作乱。)

"Ballads from the States" express passion of love without indulgence. "Minor Court Hymns" make complaints and criticisms without inciting trouble. (*Records of the Historian*)

理

Li

本义指玉石的纹理，引申而有三重含义：其一，指具体事物的样式或性质，如短长、大小、方圆、坚脆、轻重、白黑等物理属性；其二，指万事万物所遵循的普遍法则；其三，指事物的本原或本体。后两种含义与"道"相近。宋明时期的学者特别注重对"理"的阐发，以"理"为最高范畴，因此宋明时期占主导地位的学术体系被称为"理学"。

The original meaning of *li* (理) was the texture of jade; later it was extended to contain three meanings: 1) the physical forms or proprieties of things, such as length, size, shape, tensile strength, weight, and color; 2) the universal laws followed by all things and beings; and 3) the original source or ontological existence of things. The last two meanings are similar to those of Dao. Scholars of the Song and Ming dynasties were particularly interested in describing and explaining the philosophy known as *li* (理), and considered it as the highest realm, giving rise to the School of Principle which dominated academic thought in the period from the Song to the Ming dynasties.

引例 Citations：

◎物无妄然，必由其理。（王弼《周易略例·明彖》）

（事物没有随意而为的，必然会因循其理。）

Nothing happens at random; each follows its own *li* (laws). (Wang Bi: *A Brief Exposition of The Book of Changes*)

◎有物必有则，一物须有一理。（《二程遗书》卷十八）

（每一事物的存在必有其法则，但所有事物都须有万物皆同的理。）

Everything exists according to its objective law but all things must follow the common *li* (law). (*Writings of the Cheng Brothers*)

lìyòng-hòushēng 利用厚生

Make Full Use of Resources to Enrich the People

充分发挥物力的效用，使民众生活富裕。古人认为，良好的政治在于"养民"，让民众生活富足。"利用"讲的是统治者应当节俭而不奢靡浪费，使物尽其用；"厚生"讲的是减轻徭役赋税，使民众生活安宁、富裕、幸福。它是中国近代民生主义、社会主义的思想渊源之一。

The ancient Chinese believed that good governance allowed people to lead a life of plenty. The ruler should be frugal, not extravagant or wasteful. He should make good use of the country's material resources, reduce the corvée and tax burdens on the people so that they could live peaceful, prosperous, and happy lives. This belief was one of the sources of advocation for the people's livelihood and socialist thinking in modern China.

引例 Citation：

◎德惟善政，政在养民……正德、利用、厚生，惟和。(《尚书·大禹谟》)
（帝王的德行要体现为良好的施政，施政要以养育民众为目的……端正德行、物尽其用、使民众富裕，这三项工作要兼顾协调，配合得当。）

A ruler should manifest his virtue in good governance, and the goal of governance is to bring a good life to the people… The ruler should act in an upright and virtuous manner, and ensure that the country's resources are put to good use and that the people live a prosperous life. These three goals complement one another. (*The Book of History*)

liángshǐ 良史

Trustworthy Historian / Factual History

好的史家或史书，即能根据史实，客观记载书写，无所隐讳，信而有征。无论是史家，还是史书，判断其好坏的标准都在于记载历史是否客观真实。这是科学史学的首要条件。

This refers to historians or history books that record historical facts in an objective and truthful way based on evidences without covering up anything. Objectivity is the ultimate criterion for judging historians or history books in historiography.

引例 Citations：

◎然自刘向、扬雄博极群书，皆称迁有良史之材……其文直，其事核，不虚美，不隐恶，故谓之实录。(《汉书·司马迁传赞》)

（可是自从刘向、扬雄博览群书之后，都称赞司马迁具备优秀史家的资质……他行文正直合理，叙事翔实正确，不虚假赞美，不掩盖恶行，所以认为司马迁是依据史实记载的。）

However, after reading a huge number of books, Liu Xiang and Yang Xiong came to view Sima Qian as a great historian... His accounts are straightforward and reasonable, accurate and substantive, and free from false praise; they do not cover up evil deeds. Therefore Sima Qian is believed to have based his records on history. (*The History of the Han Dynasty*)

◎凡善恶必书，谓之良史。(苏鹗《苏氏演义》卷上)
(无论善恶，都照直记录书写，这就叫好史书。)

A factual history is one which records both good and evil that have happened. (Su E: *Textual Studies by Su E*)

liángzhī 良知

Liangzhi (Conscience)

人天生所具有的道德本性与道德上的认识和实践能力。"良知"一词最初由孟子（前372？—前289）提出，认为人不加思虑便能知道的便是"良知"。"良知"的具体内容包括亲爱其父母、尊敬其兄长。而亲爱父母是仁，尊敬兄长是义。"良知"说是孟子性善论的重要内容。明代的王阳明（1472—1529）提出"致良知"，进一步发展了孟子的"良知"说。他认为，"良知"就是天理，一切事物及其规律都包含在"良知"之中。将"良知"扩充到底，即能达到对一切道德真理的认识和实践。

Humans are born with innate conscience and the ability to know and act upon it. The term *liangzhi* (良知) was first used by Mencius (372?-289 BC), who believed that what man knew by instinct was *liangzhi* (knowledge of goodness). The term includes *ren* (仁), i.e. love for one's parents and *yi* (义), i.e. respect for one's elder brothers. The concept is an important component of Mencius' belief in the innate goodness of human nature. The Ming-dynasty philosopher Wang Yangming (1472-1529) raised the idea of "attaining *liangzhi*." He extended the Mencius' *liangzhi* to mean the principles of heaven, maintaining that all things under heaven and their laws were covered by *liangzhi*. With *liangzhi* being extended to its fullest (through self-cultivation and moral practice), it is possible to know and put in practice all moral truths.

引例 Citations：

◎所不虑而知者，其良知也。(《孟子·尽心上》)

(人所不加思虑便能知晓的，就是良知。)

What is known without thinking is the innate knowledge of goodness. (*Mencius*)

◎天理即是良知。(《传习录》卷下)

(天理就是良知。)

Principles of heaven and conscience are the same in essence. (*Records of Great Learning*)

liùjīng jiē shǐ 六经皆史

The Six Confucian Classics Are All About History.

　　这是古代学者提出的一个重要的学术思想命题，认为"六经"(《易》《书》《诗》《礼》《乐》《春秋》)反映的是夏、商、周三代社会、政治等现实情况的历史文本，而不是圣人刻意留下的义理说教。系统阐发这一命题的代表人物是清代学者章学诚（1738—1801）。这一命题动摇了儒家经典的神圣地位，标志着中国史学趋向自觉与独立。

The Six Confucian Classics are *The Book of Changes*, *The Book of History*, *The Book of Songs*, *The Book of Rites*, *The Book of Music*, and *The Spring and Autumn*

Annals. An important proposition put forward by scholars of late imperial China was that those are all historical texts. According to these scholars, the Six Classics are all concerned with the social and political realities of the Xia, Shang, and Zhou dynasties rather than the teachings left by ancient sages. Zhang Xuecheng (1738-1801) of the Qing Dynasty was the representative scholar to systematically expound this proposition. This view challenged the sacred status of the classics of Confucianism and marked a self-conscious and independent trend in Chinese historiography.

引例 Citation：

◎学者崇奉"六经"，以谓圣人立言以垂教，不知三代盛时，各守专官之掌故，而非圣人有意作为文章也。(章学诚《文史通义·史释》)
(学者推崇"六经"，认为圣人著书立说，是为了给后人留下垂示教训，却不知道那实际上是夏、商、周三代兴盛之时，各司其职的官员写下的制度和史实，而不是圣人有意撰写的典籍。)

Scholars worship the Six Classics and say that they are the words of sages set down to teach later generations. They do not realize that the classics are the regulations and historical facts recorded by officials in the flourishing days of the three dynasties of Xia, Shang, and Zhou. They are not the writings of ancient sages. (Zhang Xuecheng: *General Principles of History*)

liùyì 六义

The Six Basic Elements

汉代学者从治理国家与社会教化角度总结《诗经》所具有的六方面意义：

"风"是用来阐发圣贤思想对民风的教化作用,"赋"是直陈时政善恶,"比"是以类比方式委婉批评时政的不足,"兴"是借助其他美好事物来鼓励善行,"雅"是宣扬正道并作为后世的准则,"颂"是歌颂和推广美德。"六义"原本是儒家用来阐述《诗经》创作手法的术语,后来也用它来说明一切诗歌的创作方式以及文学批评的基本原则。

The six basic elements were drawn from *The Book of Songs* by scholars of the Han Dynasty to promote the state's governance, social enlightenment, and education. The six are: *feng* (ballad), which offers an insight into the influence of a sage's thinking on ordinary folk customs; *fu* (narrative), which directly states the goodness or evilness of court politics; *bi* (analogy), which criticizes mildly the inadequacies of court politics by comparing one thing with another; *xing* (association), which extols a virtue by making an indirect reference to some other laudable thing; *ya* (court hymn), which shows the proper way of acquitting oneself as a norm for posterity to follow; and *song* (eulogy), which praises and promotes virtue. All the six elements were originally used by Confucian scholars to expound on the creative techniques in *The Book of Songs*. Later, they were used to emphasize creative styles of all works of poetry. They also served as essential principles of literary criticism.

引例 Citation:

◎ 风言贤圣治道之遗化也。赋之言铺,直铺陈今之政教善恶。比,见今之失,不敢斥言,取比类以言之。兴,见今之美,嫌于媚谀,取善事以喻劝之。雅,正也,言今之正者,以为后世法。颂之言诵也、容也,诵今之德,广以美之。(《周礼·春官·大师》郑玄注)

(风是从留存的民风习俗了解圣贤的治国之道。赋是铺陈的意思,即直接陈述那些反映时政得失的事情。比是看到时政弊端,但不敢直接指斥,而以类比的方式委婉指出。兴是看到当时政治清明，担心直接赞美好似阿谀谄媚，因此借其他美好事物加以晓谕和勉励。雅是"正"的意思，讲述当今正确的做法，作为后世遵循的准则。颂是"诵"（赞颂）和"容"（仪容）的意思，即通过赞颂仪容来赞美当今君主的品德，并且推广这种美德。）

A ballad tells how to run the country via the customs and folkways that have survived through the ages. A narrative flatly states the positive and negative things in state affairs. An analogy is made when one sees a vice in court politics but dares not directly point it out; it hints at the vice by describing something similar to it. An association, in view of the clean and honest governance of the time, voices its appreciation and support through borrowing from some other commendable thing, in order to avoid arousing suspicions of unscrupulous flattery. A court hymn is related to propriety, describing something rightly done and setting norms for people of later generations to observe. A eulogy praises and promotes a reigning monarch's virtues by admiring his elegant, upright manner. (Zheng Xuan: *Annotations on The Rites of Zhou*)

měicì 美刺

Extolment and Satirical Criticism

赞美与讽刺批评。用于文学艺术领域，主要指用诗歌对统治者的品德、政令和作为进行赞美或讽刺批评。孔子（前551—前479）最早指出"诗可以怨"，强调《诗经》具有抒发不满情绪的功用，确定了诗歌创作的基本功能。汉代的诗学则迎合统治者的需要，突出诗歌歌功颂德的功能。汉代诗学作品《毛诗序》和郑玄（127—200）《诗谱序》将"美刺"确立为诗歌批评的基本原则之一，使之成为后世诗人和作家的自觉追求，是他们参与政治、干预社会生活的一种方式，从而构成中国文学的基本功用与重要特色。

This literary term is used in poetry to comment on a ruler's moral character, policies, decrees, and performance, either in praise or criticism. Confucius (551-479 BC) was the first to point out that poetry could be used to vent resentment and thus established a basic function of poetry writing by emphasizing the role *The Book of Songs* played in voicing grievances. In the Han Dynasty, however, poetry tended to be used as a vehicle for extolling the accomplishments and virtues of rulers. In "Introductions to *Mao's Version of The Book of Songs*" and Zheng Xuan's (127-200) "Preface to *On the Categories of The Book of Songs*," two influential writings on theory of poetry published during the Han Dynasty, extolment and satirical criticism was regarded as an underlying principle of poetic criticism. This principle was widely employed by poets and writers of later generations as a way of getting involved in politics and making their impact on the society. This constituted a fundamental function and an essential feature of Chinese literature.

引例 Citations：

◎ [诗]论功颂德，所以将顺其美；刺过讥失，所以匡救其恶。（郑玄《诗谱序》）

（诗歌歌颂朝廷功德，是为了让他们延续光大美好的方面；讽刺批评其过失，是为了让他们匡救改正不好的方面。）

Poems are composed to applaud the rulers to continue to do what is good by extolling their achievements and virtues, and to urge them to change the erroneous course by satirizing and criticizing their wrong doings. (Zheng Xuan: Preface to *On the Categories of The Book of Songs*)

◎汉儒言诗，不过美刺两端。（程廷祚《青溪集·诗论十三·再论刺诗》）

（汉代儒者论说诗歌，不外乎赞美歌颂与讽刺批评两方面。）

To Confucian scholars in the Han Dynasty, poetry has two basic functions: extolment and satirical criticism. (Cheng Tingzuo: *Qingxi Collection*)

mínwéibāngběn 民惟邦本

People Are the Foundation of the State.

指民众是国家的根本或基础。只有百姓安居乐业、生活稳定，国家才能安定。最早见于古文《尚书》所载大禹的训示。这与战国时代孟子（前372？—前289）提出的"民为贵，社稷次之，君为轻"，荀子（前313？—前238）提出的"水能载舟，亦能覆舟"的思想一脉相承，并由此形成儒家所推崇的"民本"思想。

This term means that the people are the essence of the state or the foundation upon which it stands. Only when people live and work in peace and contentment can the state be peaceful and stable. This saying, which first appeared in the "Old Text" version of *The Book of History* as an instruction by Yu the Great, can be traced to Mencius' (372?-289 BC) statement: "The essence of a state is the people, next come the god of land and the god of grain (which stand for state power), and the last the ruler," and Xunzi's (313?-238 BC) statement, "Just as water can float a boat, so can water overturn it." This idea gave rise to the "people first" thought advocated by Confucianism.

引例 Citation：

◎皇祖有训：民可近，不可下。民惟邦本，本固邦宁。(《尚书·五子之歌》)
（我们的祖先大禹曾经告诫说：民众可以亲近，不能认为他们卑微。民众是国家的根本，根本稳固了国家才能安宁。）

Our ancestor Yu the Great warned: (a ruler) must maintain a close relationship with the people; he must not regard them as insignificant. They are the foundation of a state, and a state can enjoy peace only when its foundation is firm. (*The Book of History*)

qì 气

Qi (Vital Force)

独立于主观意识之外的物质实体，是构成一切有形之物的原始物质材料，同时也是生命和精神得以发生和存在的基础。此外，某些思想家还为"气"赋予了道德属性。"气"没有具体的形状，永远处于运动变化之中。"气"的凝聚意味着事物的生成，"气"的消散意味着事物的消亡。"气"贯通于所有有形之物的内外。哲学意义上的"气"与常识性的"气体"概念不同，"气体"指各种非液体、非固体的存在；而从哲学层面来看，液体、固体既是有形之物，其生成、存在也是"气"凝聚的结果。

Qi (vital force) has a material existence independent of subjective consciousness and is the basic element of all physical beings. It is also the basis for the birth and existence of life and spirit. In addition, some thinkers have given a moral attribute to *qi*. *Qi* is in constant motion and change, and has no specific shape. Its concentration gives birth to a thing and its evaporation signals the end of that thing. *Qi* permeates all physical beings and their surroundings. *Qi*, as a philosophical concept, is different from what is commonly understood by the word *qi* (气), namely, air. Although things in liquid or solid form are different from things in air form, from the perspective of the ancient Chinese philosophy, their formation and existence are the results of the concentration of *qi*.

引例 Citations：

◎通天下一气耳。(《庄子·知北游》)

（贯通天下万物的就是一个"气"罢了。）

It is *qi* that permeates everything under heaven. (*Zhuangzi*)

◎天地合气，万物自生。(王充《论衡·自然》)

（天地之气相互交合，万物自然而生。）

The convergence of *qi* of heaven and that of earth gives life to all things. (Wang Chong: *A Comparative Study of Different Schools of Learning*)

qíng 情

Qing

"情"有三种不同含义：其一，泛指人的情感、欲望。"情"受外物感动而发，是人的自然本能，不是后天习得的。其二，特指人的某些情感、欲望，通常被规定为好、恶、喜、怒、哀、乐等六者，或喜、怒、哀、惧、爱、恶、欲等七者。前者也被称作"六志"或"六情"，后者被称作"七情"。其三，指情实或实情。对于前两个意义上的"情"，历代学者持有不同态度，或主张抑制"情"，或承认"情"的合理性而加以引导和安处。

The term has three different meanings. First, it means human emotions and desires, referring to the natural and instinctive reaction to external circumstances, not a learned response. Second, it refers to specific human emotions and desires, commonly known as the six human emotions: love, hatred, happiness, anger, sadness, and joy, or as the seven human emotions: happiness, anger, sadness, fear, love, hatred, and desire. Third, it means the true state of affairs, or actual situation. For centuries, scholars have had different interpretations on the first two meanings. Some advocated that emotions should be restrained or controlled, while others believed that emotions and desires were natural and should be properly guided.

引例 Citations：

◎何谓人情？喜、怒、哀、惧、爱、恶、欲，七者弗学而能。(《礼记·礼运》)

(什么叫做人之情？就是喜爱、恼怒、悲哀、恐惧、爱慕、憎恶、欲求，这七者不用学习就能产生。)

What are human emotions? They are happiness, anger, sadness, fear, love, hatred, and desire that arise instinctively. (*The Book of Rites*)

◎上好信，则民莫敢不用情。(《论语·子路》)

(地位高的人讲求诚信，则民众没有人敢不以实情相待。)

If those in high positions act in good faith, the people will not dare to conceal the truths. (*The Analects*)

qíngjǐng 情景

Sentiment and Scenery

指文学作品中摹写景物与抒发情感的相互依存和有机融合。"情"指作者内心的情感，"景"为外界景物。情景理论强调二者的交融，情无景不立，景无情不美。是宋代以后出现的文学术语，相对于早期的情物观念，情景理论更加重视景物摹写与情感抒发、创作与鉴赏过程的互相依赖与融为一体。

This term refers to the mutual dependence and integration of an author's description of scenery and objects, and his expression of feelings in his literary creation. *Qing* (情) is an author's inner feelings, and *jing* (景) refers to external scenery or an object. The theory of sentiment and scenery stresses integration of the two, maintaining that sentiment can hardly be aroused without scenery and that scenery or an object cannot be appreciated without sentiment. This term appeared in the Song Dynasty. Compared with earlier notions about sentiment and scenery, this one is more emphatic about fusing the depiction of scenery with the expression of feelings, and the process of creation with that of appreciation.

引例 Citations：

◎景无情不发，情无景不生。（范晞文《对床夜语》卷二）
（景物若没有情感的注入就不会出现在诗歌中，情感若没有景物的衬托就无从生发。）

Scenery has no place in poetry unless there are feelings for it; feelings cannot be stirred without the inspiration of scenery. (Fan Xiwen: *Midnight Dialogues Across Two Beds*)

◎情景名为二，而实不可离。神于诗者，妙合无垠。巧者则有情中景、景中情。（王夫之《姜斋诗话》卷二）
（情与景虽然名称上为二，但实际上不可分离。善于作诗的人，二者融合巧妙，看不出界限。构思精巧的则会有情中景、景中情。）

Sentiment and scenery seem to be two distinct things, but in fact they cannot be separated. A good poet knows how to integrate them seamlessly. An ingenious combination of sentiment and scenery means scenery embedded in sentiment and vice versa. (Wang Fuzhi: *Desultory Remarks on Poetry from Ginger Studio*)

qù 趣

Qu

指文学艺术作品中所表现的作者的志趣、情趣、意趣等。作者的"趣"决定他们对自然、人生的独特体验和理解，以及对作品主题的选择和作品的表现风格。"趣"是作品中无形的精神韵味，通过审美活动而体现出它的价值与品位高下。

Qu is the aspirations, emotions, and interests expressed in the work of a writer or artist. His pursuit of *qu* determines his unique perception and comprehension of nature and life. It also determines what theme he chooses for his work and how he gives expression to it. *Qu* is invisible but manifests its value and appeal through aesthetic appreciation.

引例 Citations：

◎［嵇］康善谈理，又能属文，其高情远趣，率然玄远。(《晋书·嵇康传》)
(嵇康善谈玄理，又擅长写作，他情趣高雅，率真而旷远。)

Ji Kang was good at explaining profundities and writing. He had a high style and fine taste. A forthright and broad-minded man, indeed! (*The History of the Jin Dynasty*)

◎世人所难得者唯趣。趣如山上之色，水中之味，花中之光，女中之态，虽

善说者不能下一语，唯会心者知之。……夫趣得之自然者深，得之学问者浅。（袁宏道《叙陈正甫〈会心集〉》）

（世人难以领悟的只有"趣"。"趣"好比山的颜色、水的味道、花的光彩、女人的姿容，即使擅长言辞的人也不能一句话说清楚，只有领会于心的人知道它。……趣，如果从自然之性中得来，那是深层次的"趣"；如果从学问中得来，往往是肤浅的"趣"。）

The only thing really hard to understand in the world is *qu*. *Qu* is like the hues of hills, the taste of water, the splendor of flowers, or the beauty of a woman. Even an eloquent person can hardly find words to put it clearly. Only those with empathy know it well… *Qu* that comes from nature is deep and mellow; if it comes from book learning, it is often shallow. (Yuan Hongdao: Preface to Chen Zhengfu's *Inspirations of the Mind*)

rénwén-huàchéng 人文化成

Edify the Populace to Achieve a Harmonious Society

根据社会文明的进展程度与实际状况，用合于"人文"的基本精神和原则教化民众，引导民心向善，最终实现有差等又有调和的社会秩序。"人文"指的是诗书、礼乐、法度等精神文明的创造；"化"是教化、教导（民众）并使之改变，"成"指社会文治昌明的实现。"人文化成"的核心在于强调文治，实际上是中华"文明"理想的又一表达形式。

The term is used to describe efforts to teach people essential ideals and principles of *renwen* (人文) and guide them to embrace goodness with the aim of building a harmonious – albeit hierarchical – social order, according to the level of development of a civilization and the specifics of the society. *Renwen* refers to poetry, books, social norms, music, law, and other non-material components of civilization. *Hua* (化) means to edify the populace; *cheng* (成) refers to the establishment or prosperity of rule by civil means (as opposed to force). The concept emphasizes rule by civil means, and is another expression of the Chinese concept of "civilization."

引例 Citation:

◎观乎天文，以察时变；观乎人文，以化成天下。(《周易·彖上》)
(观察日月星辰的运行状态，可以知道四季的变换；考察诗书礼乐的发展状况，可以用来教化天下百姓，实现文治昌明。)

By observing the movement of constellations, we can learn about the change of seasons; by observing development of human culture, we can enlighten the people and build a civilized society. (*The Book of Changes*)

rénzhì 人治

Rule by Man

通过规范人伦关系、道德观念和其他价值系统来治理国家和民众（与"法治"相对），是中国古代儒家政治哲学中最重要的治国理念。这种理念强调人在政治中的根本地位和作用，希望君主具备圣贤的人格，选择有道德和有才干的人治理国家，教育和感化臣民。在中国历史上，这种治国理念通常伴随着一个理想的期待，即实现君、臣、民三者之间的和谐相处，也就是"仁政"。

Rule by man, as opposed to rule by law, is the most important ruling concept in the Confucian political philosophy in ancient China. It calls for ruling a state and its people through orderly human relations, moral standards, and other value systems. Rule by man emphasizes the fundamental role and importance of people in conducting political affairs. It emphasizes that a ruler should have a lofty and noble character, select competent officials with integrity to run the state, and educate and influence the general public. In Chinese history, this concept of governance was designed to achieve a harmonious relationship between the sovereign, his officials, and his subjects, which meant "benevolent governance."

引例 Citations：

◎人治所以正人。(《礼记·大传》郑玄注)
(人治就是用来规范人伦关系的。)

Rule by man aims to regulate human relations. (Zheng Xuan: *Annotations on The Book of Rites*)

◎情性者，人治之本，礼乐所由生也。(王充《论衡·本性》)
(人治究其根本在于治理人的情感和欲望，而这也是制定礼乐的原因和依据。)

Rule by man, in the final analysis, is to regulate human emotions and desires; it is the reason and basis for developing social norms and music education. (Wang Chong: *A Comparative Study of Different Schools of Learning*)

rén 仁

***Ren* (Benevolence)**

"仁"的基本含义是爱人，进而达到人与人之间、天地万物之间一体的状态。"仁"既是道德行为的基础和依据，又是一种内在的与道德行为相应的心理意识。大体来说，"仁"有如下三重含义：其一，指恻隐之心或良心；其二，指根源于父子兄弟关系基础上的亲亲之德；其三，指天地万物一体的状态和境界。儒家将其作为最高的道德准则，并将"仁"理解为有差等的爱，即爱人以孝父母敬兄长为先，进而关爱其他家族成员，最终扩大为对天下之人的博爱。

The basic meaning of the term is love for others. Its extended meaning refers to the state of harmony among people, and the unity of all things under heaven. *Ren* (仁) constitutes the foundation and basis for moral behavior. It is also a consciousness that corresponds to the norms of moral behavior. Roughly put, *ren* has the following three implications: 1) compassion or conscience; 2) virtue of respect built upon the relationship between fathers and sons and among brothers; and 3) the unity of all things under heaven. Confucianism holds *ren* as the highest moral principle. *Ren* is taken as love in the order of first showing filial piety to one's parents and elder brothers, and then extending love and care to other members of the family, and eventually to everyone else under heaven.

引例 Citations：

◎克己复礼为仁。(《论语·颜渊》)

（克制自己的言行以符合礼的要求就是仁。）

To restrain yourself and practice propriety is benevolence. (*The Analects*)

◎仁者，爱之理，心之德也。(朱熹《论语集注》卷一)

(仁，是爱的道理，心的德性。)

Ren is the principle of love and the moral nature of human mind. (Zhu Xi: *The Analects Variorum*)

rìxīn 日新

Constant Renewal

　　天天更新。努力使自身不断更新，使民众、社会、国家不断更新，持续进步、完善，始终呈现新的气象。它是贯穿在"修齐治平"各层面的一种自强不息、不断革新进取的精神。

This term refers to an ongoing process of self-renewal, which also brings new life to the people, society, and the nation. This process features continuous progress and improvement. It represents a tenacious and innovative spirit that permeates all levels of "self-cultivation, family regulation, state governance, bringing peace to all under heaven."

引例 Citation：

◎汤之盘铭曰："苟日新，日日新，又日新。"《康诰》曰："作新民。"《诗》曰："周虽旧邦，其命惟新。"是故君子无所不用其极。(《礼记·大学》)

([商朝的开国君主]汤的浴盆上铸刻的铭文说："如果能够一天更新自己，就应天天保持更新，更新了还要再更新。"《尚书·康诰》上说："激励民众弃旧图新，去恶向善。"《诗经》上说："周虽然是古老的国家，却禀受了新的天命。"所以君子无时无处不尽心尽力革新自己。)

"If we can improve ourselves in one day, we should do so every day, and keep building on improvement," reads the inscription on the bathtub of Tang, founder of the Shang Dynasty. "People should be encouraged to discard the old and embrace the new, give up evil ideas, and live up to high moral standards," says *The Book of History*. "Though it was an ancient state, Zhou saw its future lying in continuously renewing itself," comments *The Book of Songs*. Therefore, men of virtue should strive to excel themselves in all aspects and at all times. (*The Book of Rites*)

róngcái 镕裁

Refining and Deleting

对文学作品的基本内容与词句进行提炼与剪裁，使之达到更高的水准与境界。属于文学写作的基本范畴。最早由南朝刘勰（465？—520）《文心雕龙》提出。主要指作者在写作过程中，根据所要表达的内容以及文体特点，对于创作构思中的众多素材加以提炼，同时对文辞去粗存精、删繁就简，以求得最佳表现效果。这一术语既强调文学写作的精益求精，同时也彰显了文学创作是内容与形式不断完善的过程。明清时期的戏剧创作理论也颇受其影响。

This term refers to improving a literary work by refining its basic content and making the presentation concise. Refining and deleting is a basic process in literary writing. The term was first mentioned by Liu Xie (465?-520) of the Southern Dynasties in his *The Literary Mind and the Carving of Dragons*. It means that in producing a literary work, the author should select the right elements from all the material he has, delete unnecessary parts and keep the essence, and write in a concise way to best present what he has in mind and to best suit the styles of writing. It shows that literary creation is a process of constantly striving for perfection in terms of both content and form. This idea had a great impact on the theory of theatrical writing in the Ming and Qing dynasties.

引例 Citations：

◎规范本体谓之镕，剪截浮词谓之裁。裁则芜秽不生，镕则纲领昭畅。（刘勰《文心雕龙·镕裁》）

（"镕"是规范文章的基本内容和结构，"裁"是删去多余的词句。经过剪裁，文章就没有多余杂乱的词句；经过提炼，文章就会纲目清楚、层次分明。）

Refining means to shape the basic content and structure of a literary work, while deleting means to cut off redundant words or sentences. Once done, the essay will be well structured, with a clear-cut theme. (Liu Xie: *The Literary Mind and the Carving of Dragons*)

◎［谢］艾繁而不可删，［王］济略而不可益。若二子者，可谓练镕裁而晓繁略矣。（刘勰《文心雕龙·镕裁》）

（谢艾的文章用词虽然堆砌，但都是必不可少的，不能删减；王济的语言虽然简略，但能够充分表达意思，不能增加。像这两位，可以说是精通镕裁的方法，明了繁简得当的道理了。）

Xie Ai's essays are ornate in expression yet free of unnecessary sentences or words, with nothing to be deleted. Wang Ji's writing is concise in style; it sufficiently expresses an idea without the need for using more words. Men of letters like them surely command the art of refining and deleting by using a proper amount of words and expressions. (Liu Xie: *The Literary Mind and the Carving of Dragons*)

shèjì 社稷

Gods of the Earth and the Five Grains / State / State Power

古代帝王、诸侯所祭祀的土地神和五谷神。"社"是土地神,"稷"是五谷神。土地神和五谷神是以农为本的华夏族最重要的原始崇拜物。古代君主为了祈求国事太平、五谷丰登,每年都要祭祀土地神和五谷神,"社稷"因此成为国家与政权的象征。

She (社) is the God of the Earth, and *ji* (稷 millet), represents the God of the Five Grains. Chinese kings and vassals of ancient times offered sacrifices to these gods. As the Han people depended on farming, these gods were the most important primitive objects of worship. The ancient rulers offered sacrifices to the gods of the Earth and the Five Grains every year to pray for peace and good harvests in the country. As a result, *sheji* became a symbol of the nation and state power.

引例 Citation:

◎王者所以有社稷何?为天下求福报功。人非土不立,非谷不食。土地广博,不可遍敬也;五谷众多,不可一一而祭也。故封土立社示有土尊;稷,五谷之长,故封稷而祭之也。(《白虎通义·社稷》)

(天子为何设立土地神与五谷神呢?是为了天下百姓祈求神的赐福、报答神的功德。没有土地,人就不能生存;没有五谷,人就没有食物。土地广大,不可能全都礼敬;五谷众多,不可能全都祭祀。所以封土为坛立土地神以表示土地的尊贵;稷[谷子]是五谷中最重要的粮食,所以立稷为五谷神而予以祭祀。)

Why do the Sons of Heaven worship the gods of the Earth and the Five Grains? They do so to seek blessings for all under heaven and to requite the gods' blessings. Without earth, people have nowhere to live; without grain, people have nothing to eat. The earth is too vast to be worshipped everywhere; the variety of grains is too large to be worshipped one by one. Therefore, earth altars to the God of the Earth have been set up to honor the earth; and as millet is the chief one of the five grains, it has become the God of the Five Grains and sacrifices have been instituted. (*Debates of the White Tiger Hall*)

shén 神

Shen (Spirit / Spiritual)

"神"有四种不同的含义：其一，指具有人格意义的神灵，具有超越于人力的能力。天地、山川、日月、星辰等自然事物皆有其神灵，人死后的灵魂也可以成为神灵。其二，指人的精神、心神。道教认为"神"是人的生命的主宰，因此以存神、炼神为长生之要。其三，指天地万物在阴阳的相互作用下发生的微妙不测的变化。在这个意义上，"神"常与"化"连用，合称"神化"。其四，指人所具有的神妙不可测度的生命境界。

The term has four meanings. First, it indicates a deity in a personified sense, possessing superhuman capabilities. Natural things, such as heaven and earth, mountains and rivers, sun and moon, and stars, have their deity. A human soul may also become a deity after death. Second, it indicates the human spirit and mind. Daoism considers "spirit" to be the dominating factor in human life. Therefore, maintaining and refining the spirit is most important to prolong life. Third, it indicates the subtle and unfathomable changing of all things as well as heaven and earth occurring under the interaction of yin and yang. In this sense the term is often used together with *hua* (化 change), the combination being called "divine change." Fourth, it indicates a marvelous and unfathomable realm in life attained by a person.

引例 Citations：

◎国将兴，听于民；将亡，听于神。(《左传·庄公三十二年》)
(国家将要兴盛之时，行事听从于民意；将要败亡之时，行事听从于神灵。)

The nation will prosper when people's opinions are heard and it will perish when only the will of the spirit is followed. (*Zuo's Commentary on The Spring and Autumn Annals*)

◎气有阴阳，推行有渐为化，合一不测为神。(张载《正蒙·神化》)
(气包含阴阳二气，二气的推行渐进称为化，二气交互统一不可测度的变化称为神。)

In *qi* (vital force) there are yin and yang whose gradual operation means change. The unpredictable interaction and unity of yin and yang is what is called spirit. (Zhang Zai: *Enlightenment Through Confucian Teachings*)

◎圣而不可知之之谓神。(《孟子·尽心下》)
(圣德到了神妙不可测度的境界称作"神"。)

Being sage beyond understanding, that is called divine. (*Mencius*)

shénsī 神思

Imaginative Contemplation

文艺创作过程中的一种精神状态，指的是作者在饱满的情感驱动下，超越时间与空间的限制，进入到自由想象或特殊的灵感状态，最后通过特定的文学艺术形象和语言而传达出来，创作出自然而美好的文艺作品。这一术语，在魏晋南北朝的文艺理论中得到广泛运用，南朝刘勰（465？—520）《文心雕龙》对此有专门论述。"神思"是文艺创作中一种独特的心理活动，不同于其他认识活动。

The term refers to a state of mind in the process of literary and artistic creation. It suggests that the author, fully inspired by emotions, transcends the constraint of time and space, and enters into a state of free imagination or a special mood for literary and artistic creation, before producing a natural and beautiful work of literature or art, either in language or in imagery. This term was popularly used in literary and artistic theories of the Wei, Jin, and Southern and Northern dynasties. Liu Xie (465?-520) of the Southern Dynasties devoted one chapter especially to this term in *The Literary Mind and the Carving of Dragons*. Imaginative contemplation is the unique mental activity in literary and artistic creation, different from other cognitive activities.

引例 Citations：

◎古人云："形在江海之上，心存魏阙之下。"神思之谓也。文之思也，其神远矣。（刘勰《文心雕龙·神思》）

（古人说："身在民间，心却想着朝廷。"这说的就是神思。文章写作时的想象和思绪，其神奇是可以超越时空的呀！）

An ancient saying goes, "Though he lives among the common folks, deep in his heart he concerns himself with affairs of the imperial court." This is called imaginative contemplation. When one writes, his imaginations and thoughts may transcend time and space. (Liu Xie: *The Literary Mind and the Carving of Dragons*)

◎属（zhǔ）文之道，事出神思，感召无象，变化不穷。(《南齐书·文学传论》)

（写文章的规律，来自于神思，人对万物的感触没有形迹，变化无穷。）

The guiding principles for literary creation come from imaginative contemplation. Man's feelings and thoughts about the external world are formless and highly changeable. (*The History of Qi of the Southern Dynasties*)

shēng yī wú tīng, wù yī wú wén 声一无听，物一无文

A Single Note Does Not Compose a Melodious Tune, Nor Does a Single Color Make a Beautiful Pattern.

单一声响不构成动听的旋律，单一颜色不构成美丽的花纹。其本质强调文学艺术的美在于多样性的统一与和谐，只有在多样性的统一与和谐中才能创造美。这一命题后来构成中国古代文艺理论的重要原则，推动文艺的繁荣与发展。

This statement suggests that the beauty of literature and art lies in the unity and harmony of diverse elements. It became an important principle in ancient Chinese theories on literature and art, and facilitated the development of literature and art.

引例 Citations：

◎声一无听，物一无文，味一无果，物一不讲。(《国语·郑语》)
（单一声响不能构成动听的旋律，单一颜色不能构成美丽的花纹，单一味道不能成为美食，单一事物无法进行比较。）

A single note does not compose a melodious tune; a single color does not form a beautiful pattern; a single flavor does not make a delicious meal; and a single thing has nothing to compare with. (*Discourses on Governance of the States*)

◎五色杂而成黼黻（fǔfú），五音比而成韶夏，五情发而为辞章，神理之数也。(刘勰《文心雕龙·情采》)
（五色交错而成灿烂的锦绣，五音排列而组织成悦耳的乐章，五情抒发而成动人的辞章，这是自然的道理。）

When silk threads of various colors are woven together, a beautiful piece of embroidery is created. When the five musical notes are properly arranged, a beautiful melody is composed. When the five emotions are forcefully expressed, a beautiful piece of writing is created. This is all too natural and obvious. (Liu Xie: *The Literary Mind and the Carving of Dragons*)

shèng 圣

Sage / Sageness

人所能达到的最高品德；也指具有这种最高品德的人，即"圣人"。"圣"一般与"智"相对而言，"智"是对"人道"的把握，而"圣"则是对"天道"的把握。由于具"圣"德之人能够把握"天道"，因此在人伦日用中通达无碍。

The term refers to the highest realm of human integrity and morality, hence one who has reached this state is a sage. It is often used in relation to "intelligence," since an intelligent man understands the way of man, while a sage understands the way of heaven. Thus a sage with knowledge of the way of heaven will interact successfully with other people.

引例 Citations：

◎闻君子道，聪也。闻而知之，圣也。圣人知天道也。(郭店楚简《五行》)
(听闻君子的准则，可谓之"聪"。听闻而能知晓其义，可谓之"圣"。圣人知晓"天道"。)

He who listens to the principles of men of virtue is wise; he who not only listens but also understands them is a sage. The sage understands the way of heaven. (*Wuxing*, from the bamboo slips unearthed from a Chu State tomb at Guodian)

◎孔子，圣之时者也。(《孟子·万章下》)
(孔子，是圣人中把握时运的人。)

Confucius was a sage who was able to seize the opportunity of his era. (*Mencius*)

shī yán zhì 诗言志

Poetry Expresses Aspirations.

诗歌表达作者内心的志向。"志"指诗歌作品中所表达的作者的内心志向、思想，兼及情感因素。"诗言志"最先见于儒家经典《尚书·舜典》，是中国诗论的"开山纲领"（朱自清语），经过历代诗论家的演绎，其蕴涵不断得以丰富，并由此确立了中国文论关于文学特征的基本观念。

A poem expresses aspirations in one's heart. *Zhi* (志) here means the author's aspirations, emotions, and thoughts. The concept of "poetry expressing aspirations," first seen in the Confucian classic *The Book of History,* was hailed by Zhu Ziqing as the "manifesto" of Chinese poetry. Enriched by poetry critics through the generations, it was later established as a basic concept in Chinese literary criticism.

引例 Citations：

◎诗言志，歌永言。(《尚书·舜典》)
（诗是表达内心志向的，歌是用语言来吟唱的。）

Poems express aspirations deep in one's heart, whereas songs are verses for chanting. (*The Book of History*)

◎诗者，志之所之也，在心为志，发言为诗。(《毛诗序》)
（诗是内心情感意志的表达，藏在心里就是情感意志，用语言把它表达出来就是诗歌。）

Poetry is an expression of a person's feelings and aspirations. When hidden in his heart, it is just his feelings and aspirations. When put forth through the medium of words, it becomes what is known as poetry. (Introductions to *Mao's Version of The Book of Songs*)

shī yuán qíng 诗缘情

Poetry Springs from Emotions.

诗歌缘于诗人内心的情感。西晋陆机（261—303）《文赋》提出，诗人情动于心，而后才有诗歌创作。"诗缘情"说与"诗言志"说互为补充，强调文学的抒情性与审美特征，表现出魏晋时代文学观念的变迁。因此，"诗缘情"也成为中国古代关于诗歌与文学本质看法的另一代表观点。

Poems originate from the poet's heart-felt feelings. Lu Ji (261-303) of the Western Jin Dynasty said in "The Art of Writing" that a poet must have a surge of feeling deep in his heart before he could create a poem. This view, complementing the concept of "poetry expressing aspirations," stresses the lyrical and aesthetic nature of literary works and echoes the evolution of literary tastes during the Wei and Jin dynasties. "Poetry springing from emotions" represents another viewpoint on the nature of poetry and literature in ancient China.

引例 Citations：

◎诗缘情而绮靡。（陆机《文赋》）

（诗歌源于情感因而形式华丽好看。）

Poetry, springing from emotions, reads beautifully in its form of expression. (Lu Ji: The Art of Writing)

◎人禀七情，应物斯感，感物吟志，莫非自然。（刘勰《文心雕龙·明诗》）

（人具有喜、怒、哀、惧、爱、恶、欲等七种情感，受到外物的刺激而心有所感，心有所感而吟咏情志，所有的诗歌都出于自然情感。）

People have the seven emotions of joy, anger, sadness, fear, love, loathing and desire. He expresses his feelings and aspirations in a poetical way when he is stimulated by the external world and his heart is touched. All poems come from natural emotions. (Liu Xie: *The Literary Mind and the Carving of Dragons*)

shǐcái-sāncháng 史才三长

Three Strengths of a Good Historian

指修史或治史的人必须具备史才、史学、史识等三项专长。是唐代著名史学理论家刘知几（jī，661—721）提出的史学观点。"史才"指史书撰述能力；"史学"指丰富的历史知识和资料；"史识"指分析和评判历史的思想见识。刘知几认为，修史或治史的人必须同时具备这三种能力，其中"史识"最为重要。

According to the renowned historiographer Liu Zhiji (661-721) of the Tang Dynasty, those who study and write history must have three strengths, namely, the ability to compose historical works, rich knowledge of history and historical materials, and deep insight that enables them to analyze and evaluate history. Liu believed that deep insight in analyzing and commenting on history was the most important of the three qualifications.

引例 Citation：

◎ 史才须有三长……三长，谓才也，学也，识也。（《旧唐书·刘子玄传》）
（所谓"史才"必须具备三方面专长……三方面专长指的是"史才""史学""史识"。）

A historian must have three strengths… The three strengths are talent, learning, and insight. (*The Old Tang History*)

shūyuàn 书院

Classical Academy

唐宋至明清时期出现的一种文化教育机构，是私人或官府所设的聚徒传授、研究学问的场所，兼具教学、研究、藏书等多种功能。它渊源于佛教禅林和私人藏书楼，萌生于唐，兴盛于宋。南宋初年，朱熹（1130—1200）、张栻（shì，1133—1180）、吕祖谦（1137—1181）、陆九渊（1139—1193）等学者兴办书院，使之成为讲学及学派活动的基地。书院独立于官学之外，多设于环境宁静优美之地，由名师硕儒主持，追求学术自由与创新，注重言传身教、人格塑造，不图科举功名。南宋末年，书院逐步趋于官学，并与科举制度贯通。书院的兴衰与宋明理学的兴衰互为表里。1901年清政府下令书院全部改为学堂。书院前后存在一千多年，对中国古代教育和文化发展、推动中国文化走向海外产生过重大影响。

Classical academies were cultural and educational institutions that existed in China from the Tang and Song dynasties through the Ming and Qing dynasties. They were established either by the public or the government to serve the multiple purposes of education, research, and library service. Their origins were Buddhist monasteries and private libraries in the Tang Dynasty. Classical academies flourished in the Song Dynasty. In the early years of the Southern Song Dynasty, Zhu Xi (1130-1200), Zhang Shi (1133-1180), Lü Zuqian (1137-1181), Lu Jiuyuan (1139-1193), and some other scholars established academies that served as teaching and research centers of their respective schools of thought. The academies were independent of government schools and were located mostly in tranquil and scenic places. Under the supervision of learned Confucian scholars, the academies pursued academic freedom and innovation. Teachers taught by both precept and example, and laid stress on shaping their students' moral character, rather than encouraging them to win degrees in the imperial civil examination system. By the end of the Southern Song Dynasty, however, the academies became increasingly government-oriented and were linked with the imperial civil examination system. The rise and decline of the academies was in harmony with the rise and decline of the School of Principle during the Song and Ming dynasties.

In 1901 the Qing government ordered all the academies be changed to schools in modern sense. Having existed for more than 1,000 years, the academies greatly helped develop traditional Chinese culture and education, and convey Chinese culture abroad.

引例 Citation：

◎其他先儒过化之地，名贤经行之所，与好事之家出钱粟赡学者，并立为书院。(《元史·选举志一·学校》)

(其他先世儒者曾经教化百姓、著名贤士生活并留下事迹的地方，以及那些乐意出钱粮供养学者的富裕人家，都可成为创设书院的缘由。)

Places where earlier Confucian scholars taught, or where distinguished men of virtue lived and left behind stories and legacies, or wealthy families who were willing to support scholars with money and food, could all contribute to the establishment of classical academies. (*The History of the Yuan Dynasty*)

shùntiān-yìngrén 顺天应人

Follow the Mandate of Heaven and Comply with the Wishes of the People

顺应上天的旨意和民众的意愿。"天"即"天命",指上天旨意。古人认为,有德行的人秉承上天意志而确立政权,成为君主,故称为"天命"。"人"指人心、民意。它与西方"君权神授"思想相似,但它还强调人心、民意,体现了人本思想。在古代它常被用于称扬新朝代的建立和社会重大变革的实施,以表明其正当性、合法性。

The ancient Chinese believed that virtuous men followed the will of heaven in establishing a political regime and becoming its sovereigns; hence their success came from the mandate of heaven. This thought is similar to the Western notion of the divine right of kings; but it also emphasizes the wishes and will of the people, or people-centered thinking. In ancient China, this phrase was often used in praise of the founding of a new dynasty, and the implementation of major social reforms to justify its legitimacy.

引例 Citation：

◎天地革而四时成。汤武革命,顺乎天而应乎人。(《周易·彖下》)
(天地有阴阳的变化而形成一年四季。商汤、周武王变革天命 [推翻旧政权,建立新政权],是顺应了上天的旨意和人民的意愿。)

Changes of yin and yang in heaven and earth give rise to the four seasons. Following the mandate of heaven and complying with the wishes of the people, King Tang and King Wu overthrew old regimes and established the Shang and Zhou dynasties respectively. (*The Book of Changes*)

tàijí 太极

Taiji (The Supreme Ultimate)

"太极"有三种不同的含义：其一，指世界的本原。但古人对"太极"的世界本原之义又有不同理解：或以"太极"为混沌未分的"气"或"元气"；或以之为世界的普遍法则，即"道"或"理"；或以之为"无"。其二，占筮术语。指奇（—）偶（――）两画尚未推演确定或蓍草混一未分的状态，是卦象的根源。其三，指空间的最高极限。

Taiji (the supreme ultimate) has three different meanings. First, it refers to the origin of the world. The ancient Chinese saw it either as *qi* (vital force) or *yuanqi* (primordial vital force) that permeates the chaotic world, or as a universal principle, i.e. Dao or *li* (理), or as *wu* (无). Second, it is used as a term of divination, referring to the initial state before divinatory numbers, the odd number one (written as —) and the even number two (written as ――), are applied or before the yarrow stems are divided. Divination is conducted on the basis of *taiji*. Third, it stands for the highest point or boundary of space.

引例 Citations：

◎《易》始于太极，太极分而为二，故生天地。(《易纬·乾凿度》卷上)
(《易》起始于太极，太极一分为二，因此生成了天地。)

Changes evolve from *taiji*, which gives rise to two primal forces of yin and yang. They in turn give birth to heaven and earth. (*An Alternative Explanation of The Book of Changes*)

◎总天地万物之理，便是太极。(《朱子语类》卷九十四)

（总合天地万物的理，便是太极。）

Taiji is the overriding law of all things, as well as heaven and earth. (*Classified Conversations of Master Zhu Xi*)

tàixué 太学

Imperial Academy

　　由朝廷创办的设于京师的最高学府和最高教育行政机构。西周时期即有"太学"之名，但真正创设是在汉武帝（前156—前87）时期。太学的教授称"博士"，由精通儒家经典、有丰富教学经验、德才兼备的著名学者担任；学生称"博士弟子""太学生"等，最多时达万人。其后至明清，中央政府一般都在京师设立太学，或设与太学相同职能的教育机构，名称不一，具体制度也有变化。作为官立的中央最高学府，它和地方教育机构、私人教育组织一起构成了中国古代完备的教育体系。它对于传播儒家经典和以儒家为主的主流价值观起到了重要作用。

The imperial academy was the highest educational institution and educational administrative department in feudal China. The term first appeared in the Western Zhou Dynasty, but the first imperial academy was not officially established until 124 BC during the reign of Emperor Wu (156-87 BC) of the Han Dynasty. Teachers of the imperial academy were called "grand academicians" (literarily "scholars of broad learning"). They were well versed in Confucian classics, had rich teaching experience, and possessed both moral integrity and professional competence. Their students were called "students of the imperial academy" or "students of the grand academicians." At its peak the imperial academy had 10,000 students.

The central governments of all subsequent dynasties, including the Ming and Qing, had an imperial academy or a similar institution of education, usually located in the capital. It had different names and systems in different dynasties. The imperial academy, the top institution of learning run by the central government, along with local institutions of education and private schools, formed a complete education system in ancient China. They were significant in disseminating the Confucian classics and ancient China's mainstream values with Confucianism as its main school of thought.

引例 Citation：

◎臣愿陛下兴太学，置明师，以养天下之士。(《汉书·董仲舒传》)

(我希望陛下兴办太学，安排精通经书的老师，来培养天下的读书人。)

May I propose Your Majesty establish an imperial academy where teachers well versed in the Confucian classics can train students from all over the country. (*The History of the Han Dynasty*)

tǐxìng 体性

Style and Temperament

　　作品风格与作者个性的统一与结合。是关于文学风格的重要术语。"体"在这里主要指文章风格，"性"指作者个性因素。源出于南朝刘勰(465？—520)《文心雕龙·体性》。该文提出作者的个性特点与文章风格有着内在的关联，文如其人。这启发了后人从作者个性着眼去分析文学作品不同的风格类型，奠定了中国古代文学风格论的基本思想。

This is an important term about literary style that stresses the unity and integration of the styles of writings with the temperaments of their authors. The term originated by Liu Xie (465?-520) of the Southern Dynasties in his *The Literary Mind and the Carving of Dragons*. One chapter of the book discusses how the styles of writings are related to the temperaments of the writers, and argues that the writings truly reflect the temperaments of their authors. This has encouraged later generations to analyze different styles of literary works based on the authors' temperaments and became a basic line of thought on ancient Chinese literary style.

引例 Citations：

◎夫情动而言形，理发而文见（xiàn）。盖沿隐以至显，因内而符外者也。然才有庸俊，气有刚柔，学有浅深，习有雅郑；并情性所铄（shuò），陶染所凝，是以笔区云谲（jué），文苑波诡者矣。（刘勰《文心雕龙·体性》）
（情感激发而形成语言，道理表达便体现为文章。也就是将隐藏在内心的情和理逐渐彰显、由内至外的过程。不过人的才华有平凡和杰出之分，气禀有阳刚与阴柔之别，学识有浅深之异，习性有雅正和鄙俗之差。这些都是由人的先天情性所造就，并由后天的熏陶积聚而成，所以他们的创作奇谲如风云变幻，文章诡秘似海涛翻转。）

When emotions stir, they take the form of language. When ideas emerge, they are expressed in writings. Thus the obscure becomes manifest and the internal feelings pour into the open. However, talent may be mediocre or outstanding, temperament masculine or feminine, learning deep or shallow, upbringing refined or vulgar. All this results from differences in nature and nurture. Hence the unusual cloud-like variations in the realm of writing and the mysterious wave-like undulations in the garden of literature. (Liu Xie: *The Literary Mind and the Carving of Dragons*)

◎故性格清彻者音调自然宣畅，性格舒徐者音调自然疏缓，旷达者自然浩荡，雄迈者自然壮烈，沉郁者自然悲酸，古怪者自然奇绝。有是格，便有是调，皆情性自然之谓也。莫不有情，莫不有性，而可以一律求之哉？（李贽《读律肤说》）

（所以那些性情开朗透明的人所作诗的音律自然直接流畅，性情迟缓的人所作诗的音律自然疏朗宽缓，性情旷达的人所作诗的音律自然磊落浩荡，性情雄奇豪迈的人所作诗的音律自然强劲壮烈，性情沉郁的人所作诗的音律自然悲凉酸楚，性情古怪的人所作诗的音律自然不同寻常。有什么性情，便有什么音律，这都是个性气质所自然决定的。人莫不有情感，莫不有个性，怎么可以用一个音律标准去要求所有的诗歌呢？）

So it is natural that those with an open and easy-going temperament create poems with tonal rhythms that are direct, smooth, and easy to understand; those with a slow temperament write in relaxed tonal rhythms; those with a broad mind, magnificent and uninhibited; those with a heroic character, powerful and gallant; those with a depressed personality, sad and miserable; those with a weird temperament, out of the ordinary. Temperament decides the tonal rhythms of an author's writings. People have their own emotions and personalities. How can all the poems be judged by the same standard for tonal rhythms? (Li Zhi: My Understanding of Poetic Genre)

tǐyòng 体用

Ti and Yong

"体用"有三种不同含义：其一，形体、实体为"体"，形体、实体的功能、作用为"用"。其二，事物的本体为"体"，本体的显现、运用为"用"。其三，行事、行为的根本原则为"体"，根本原则的具体施用为"用"。在"体用"对待的关系中，"体"是基础，"用"是依赖于"体"的。

Ti (体) and yong (用) can be understood in three different ways: 1) a physical thing and its functions or roles; 2) the ontological existence of a thing and its expression and application; and 3) the fundamental code of conduct, and its observance. In any ti–yong relationship, ti provides the basis on which yong depends.

引例 Citations：

◎天者定体之名，乾者体用之称。(《周易·乾》孔颖达正义)
（"天"是确定实体的名称，"乾"是表现实体之功用的名称。）

Tian (天) means heaven in the physical sense, while qian (乾) means its functions and significance. (Kong Yingda: *Correct Meaning of The Book of Changes*)

◎至微者理也，至著者象也。体用一源，显微无间。(程颐《程氏易传·序》)
（最隐微的是理，最显著的是象。作为本体的理和作为现象的象出自同一来源，显著与隐微之间没有差别。）

What is most subtle is li (理), while what is most conspicuous is xiang (象). Li as the ontological existence and xiang as its manifestation are of the same origin; there is no difference between them. (Cheng Yi: *Cheng Yi's Commentary on The Book of Changes*)

tiān 天

Tian (Heaven)

"天"是中国古代思想中具有神圣性和终极意义的一个概念。主要有三种不同的含义：其一，指自然意义上的天空或人世之外的整个自然界，其运行呈现出一定的规律和秩序。其二，指主宰万物的具有人格意志的神灵。其三，指万事万物所遵循的普遍法则，同时也是人的心性、道德以及社会和政治秩序的依据。

Tian (天) is a sacred and fundamental concept in ancient Chinese philosophy. It has three different meanings. The first is the physical sky or the entirety of nature (not including human society), the operations of which manifest certain laws and order. The second refers to a spiritual being, which possesses an anthropomorphic will and governs everything in the universe. The third denotes the universal law, which is observed by all things and beings, and which is also the basis of human nature, morality, and social and political orders.

引例 Citations：

◎天行有常，不为尧存，不为桀亡。(《荀子·天论》)
（天的运行有其常道，不因为尧在位而存在，不因为桀在位而消失。）

Nature's ways are constant. They did not exist because Yao was on the throne or disappear because Jie was the ruler. (*Xunzi*)

◎上天孚佑下民。(《尚书·汤诰》)
（上天信任并保佑百姓。）

Heaven trusts and blesses the people. (*The Book of History*)

◎天者，理也。(《二程遗书》卷十一)

（天就是宇宙的普遍法则。）

Heaven is the overarching law of the universe. (*Writings of the Cheng Brothers*)

tiānxià 天下

Tianxia (All Under Heaven)

古多指天子统治范围内的全部土地及统治权。古人认为，大夫的统治范围是"家"，诸侯的统治范围是"国"，天子的统治范围是"天下"。"天下"字面义是"普天之下"，实质指天子统治或名义之下的"家国"统合体所覆盖的全部疆域，并包括天下所有的人及国家的统治权。后演变指全民族或全世界。

This term referred mainly to all the land under the name of the Son of Heaven and the right to rule on such land. The ancient Chinese held that the rule of senior officials was over their enfeoffed land, and that of dukes and princes was over feudal states. The rule of the Son of Heaven was over all the land. Literally, *tianxia* (天下) means "all under heaven." It actually refers to all the territory embracing the enfeoffed land and feudal states under the rule or in the name of the Son of Heaven, as well as all the subjects and the right to rule. The term has later evolved to refer to the whole nation or the whole world.

引例 Citations：

◎溥天之下，莫非王土；率土之滨，莫非王臣。(《诗经·小雅·北山》)

（普天之下，无一不是天子的土地；四海之内，无一不是天子的臣民。）

All land under heaven falls within the domain of the Son of Heaven; all those on this land are his subjects. (*The Book of Songs*)

◎大道之行也，天下为（wéi）公。选贤与能，讲信修睦。(《礼记·礼运》)

（大道实行的时代，天下为天下人所共有。品德高尚、才能突出的人被选拔出来管理社会，人与人之间讲求诚实与和睦。）

When the Great Way prevails, the world belongs to all the people. People of virtue and competence are chosen to govern the country; honesty is valued and people live in harmony. (*The Book of Rites*)

◎天下兴亡，匹夫有责。(梁启超《痛定罪言》三)

（天下的兴盛与衰亡，[关乎到每个人，因此]每个人都有责任。）

The rise and fall of a nation is the concern of every individual. (Liang Qichao: Painful Reflections on Current Affairs Despite Possible Incrimination)

wáng 王

King

本为夏、商、周三代天子的称号，春秋以后周天子一统天下的局面遭到破坏，至战国时期列国君主皆可称王。秦汉以后，"王"一般是皇帝对自己直系男性亲属的最高封爵。在儒家特别是孔孟的政治哲学论述中，"王"一方面代表上天的旨意，具有至高无上的权力；另一方面又被赋予了极强的道德特质和政治理想。儒家认为，用仁义治理或统一天下、以道德手段使天下人都来归顺叫做"王（wàng）"，依靠仁义道德形成天下一统的政治局面叫做"王道"。

King was originally the title for the "Son of Heaven," namely, the country's supreme ruler in the Xia, Shang and Zhou dynasties. From the Spring and Autumn Period onward, the power of the Zhou court gradually weakened and the kingdom disintegrated. By the time of the Warring States Period, any monarch could call himself a king. Up to the Qin and Han dynasties, king became the highest title granted by the emperor to a male member of the imperial family. In the political philosophical discourse of Confucianism, especially in the works of Confucius (551-479 BC) and Mencius (372?-289 BC), a king represents heaven's will and therefore ought to have supreme, unchallengeable power; at the same time, he is imbued with a high moral attribute and political ideals. According to Confucianism, to be a king is to unify or govern the country with benevolence and righteousness, or to win over people by morally justified means. Likewise, the pursuit of the kingly way means using benevolent and righteous means to unify and govern the country.

引例 Citation：

◎天下归之之谓王，天下去之之谓亡。(《荀子·正论》)

（天下人归顺他，就可以称王；天下人抛弃他，就只会灭亡。）

He to whom the people swear allegiance can rule as a king; he perishes when the people desert him. (*Xunzi*)

wángdào 王道

Kingly Way (Benevolent Governance)

儒家提倡的以仁义治理天下、以德服人的政治主张（与"霸道"相对）。

上古贤明帝王多以仁德治国，至战国时代孟子（前372？—前289）将其提升为政治理念，提出国君应当以仁义治国，在处理国与国之间的关系时要以德服人，这样才能得到民众拥护，统一天下。它是中华民族崇尚"文明"、反对武力和暴政的具体体现。

Confucianism advocates the political principle of governing the country through benevolence and winning people's support through virtue as opposed to rule by force. Enlightened kings and emperors of ancient times governed the country primarily through benevolence and virtue. In the Warring States Period, Mencius (372?-289 BC) advocated this idea as a political concept: Only by governing the state with benevolence and righteousness, and by handling state-to-state relations on the basis of virtue, can a ruler win popular support and subsequently unify the country. The kingly way or benevolent governance epitomizes the Chinese people's respect for "civilization" and their opposition to the use of force and tyranny.

引例 Citations：

◎无偏无党，王道荡荡。(《尚书·洪范》)
（公正而不偏私结党，圣王之道宽广无边。）

By upholding justice without any partiality or bias, the kingly way is inclusive and boundless. (*The Book of History*)

◎以力假仁者霸，霸必有大国；以德行仁者王，王不待大……以力服人者，非心服也，力不赡也；以德服人者，中心悦而诚服也，如七十子之服孔子也。(《孟子·公孙丑上》)
（凭借强力而假托仁义的人可以称霸，称霸一定以大国作基础；依靠德行施行仁义的人可以称王，称王却不一定非大国不可……依靠强力使他人服从，他们并不是真心服从,而是力量不足以抗拒;通过德行而令人服从,他们是内心喜悦而诚心服从,就像孔子的七十余位弟子饮服孔子那样。)

One who seizes throne by force in the name of benevolence and justice needs a big state as his power base. One who ascends the throne by upholding morality and benevolence may not necessarily have a big state as his base… Coercion can bring people in line not because they are willing, but because they do not have the strength to resist; it is virtue that will persuade others to gladly and willingly follow, just as in the case of Confucius' seventy disciples who followed him out of true conviction. (*Mencius*)

wéizhèng-yǐdé 为政以德

Governance Based on Virtue

以道德原则执掌国政、治理国家。孔子(前551—前479)在西周统治者一向秉承的"明德慎罚"的基础上提出了为后世儒家所遵循的"德政"理念。"德政"与"威刑"相对。"为政以德"并非不要刑法,而是突出强调道德对政治的决定作用,将道德教化视为治国的根本原则与方法。

Governance of a state should be guided by virtue. Confucius (551-479 BC) expounded this philosophy – which his followers in later eras promoted – on the basis of the approach advocated by the rulers in the Western Zhou Dynasty that prized high moral values and the virtue of being cautious in meting out punishment. Governance based on virtue stands in contrast to rule by use of harsh punishment as a deterrent. It does not, however, exclude the use of punishment, but rather highlights the decisive role of virtue in governance, and regards moral edification both as the fundamental principle and the essential means for achieving good governance.

引例 Citation：

◎为政以德，譬如北辰居其所，而众星共（gǒng）之。(《论语·为政》)
（以道德教化来治理政事，就像北极星位于天空一定的方位，而众星都环绕着它运行。）

Governance based on virtue is like the North Star taking its place in the sky, while all the other stars revolve around it. (*The Analects*)

wénmíng 文明

Wenming (Civilization)

指社会文治教化彰明昌盛的状态。"文"指"人文"，指礼乐教化以及与此相关的有差等又有调和的社会秩序；"明"即光明、昌明、通达之义。中华民族崇文而不尚武，自古便将文治教化的彰明昌盛作为自己的最高理想和追求，并以此作为评判异国他域政治是否清明的重要标准。

This term refers to a thriving, prosperous, and perceptibly refined society in which people behave in a cultured fashion. *Wen* (文) refers to the arts and humanities, including social norms, music education, moral cultivation, and a social order that is hierarchical yet harmonious. *Ming* (明) means bright, prosperous, and highly civilized. The Chinese nation has always preferred *wen* to *wu* (武 force). This is the loftiest ideal pursued by the Chinese nation since ancient times. It was also the criterion by which to judge whether the governance of a nation was well conducted.

引例 Citation：

◎文明之世，销锋铸耜（sì）。（焦赣（gòng）《易林·节之颐》）
（文明时代，销毁兵器而铸造农具。）

In a civilized society weapons are destroyed to make farming tools. (Jiao Gong: *Annotations on The Book of Changes*)

wénqì 文气

Wenqi

　　作品中所表现出的作者的精神气质与个性特点。是作家的内在精神气质与作品外在的行文气势相融合的产物。"气"原指构成天地万物始初的基本元素，用在文论中，既指作家的精神气质，也指这种精神气质在作品中的具体表现。人禀天地之气而形成不同的个性气质，表现在文学创作中，便形成不同的文气，呈现出独特的风格特点及气势强弱、节奏顿挫等。

Wenqi (文气) is the personality an author demonstrates in his works, and is a fusion of his innate temperament and the vitality seen in his works. Originally, *qi* (气) referred to the basic element in the initial birth and formation of all things, as well as heaven and earth. In literary criticism, it refers to an author's distinctive individuality and its manifestation in his writings. Humans are believed to develop different characters and traits endowed by the *qi* of heaven and earth. Reflected in literary creation, such different characters and traits naturally find expression in distinctive styles and varying degrees of vigor as well as rhythm and cadence.

引例 Citations：

◎文以气为主，气之清浊有体，不可力强而致。（曹丕《典论·论文》）
（文章由作家的"气"为主导，气有清气、浊气两种形态[决定人的气质优劣与材质高下]，不是强行可以获得的。）

Literary writing is governed by *qi*. Either clear or murky, *qi* determines the temperament of a writer, refined or vulgar, and his talent, high or low. *Qi* cannot be acquired. (Cao Pi: On Literary Classics)

◎气盛则言之短长与声之高下者皆宜。（韩愈《答李翊（yì）书》）
（文章的气势很强，那么句子长短搭配和音调的抑扬顿挫自然都会恰当。）

If a writer has a strong inner flow of *qi*, the length of his sentences will be well-balanced, and his choice of tone and cadence will just be right. (Han Yu: A Letter of Response to Li Yi)

wényǐzàidào 文以载道

Literature Is the Vehicle of Ideas.

　　儒家关于文学与道关系的论述。"文"指的是文学创作及作品；"道"指的是作品中的思想内容，但古代文学家与理学家将"道"主要理解为儒家所倡导的思想和道德。中唐时期古文运动的领袖韩愈（768—824）等人提出"文以明道"的观点，认为文章主旨应合乎并发挥圣人的经典。宋代理学家周敦颐（1017—1073）进一步发展为"文以载道"，提出文学像"车"，"道"即是车上运载的货物，文学不过是用以传播儒家之"道"的手段和工具。这一命题的价值在于强调文学的社会功用，强调文学作品应该言之有物、有正确的思想内容。但它轻视文学自身的审美特性，故后来受到重视文学自身价值的思想家与文学家的反对。

This term is a Confucian statement about the relationship between literature and ideas. *Wen* (文) refers to literary creations and works, while *dao* (道) refers to the ideas conveyed by literary works. Writers and philosophers in ancient China explicated these ideas as Confucian thought and ethics. Han Yu (768-824), leader of the mid-Tang-dynasty Classical Prose Movement advocating the prose style of the Qin and Han dynasties, and some others proposed that the purpose of writings should be in line with the classics of the ancient sages as well as promote them. Zhou Dunyi (1017-1073), a neo-Confucian philosopher of the Song Dynasty, expounded the principle of literature serving as a vehicle of ideas. He concluded that literature was like a vehicle while ideas were like goods loaded on it, and that literature was nothing but a means and a vehicle to convey Confucian ideas. This theory was valuable because it stressed the social role of literature and emphasized that writers should know what they were writing about to ensure that their works conveyed correct ideas. However, it underestimated the aesthetic value of literature and later met opposition from thinkers and writers who emphasized the value of literature per se.

引例 Citation：

◎文所以载道也。轮辕饰而人弗庸，徒饰也，况虚车乎？文辞，艺也；道德，实也。(周敦颐《通书·文辞》)
(文章是用来承载思想和道德的。车轮与车辕过度装饰而没人使用，白白装饰了，更何况那些派不上用场的车呢？文辞，只是一种技艺，而道德才是文章的实质。)

Writings are meant to convey ideas and ethics. When vehicles are not used, even if the wheels and shafts are excessively decorated, it is simply a waste. Fine language is only a means for writing, whereas ethics are the essence of writings. (Zhou Dunyi: *The Gist of Confucian Thought*)

wúwéi 无为

Non-action

"为"的一种状态。道家以"有为"与"无为"相对。所谓"有为",一般是指统治者把自己的意志强加给他人或世界,不尊重或不顺应万物的本性。"无为"的意义与之相反,包含三个要点:其一,权力通过自我节制的方式遏制自己的干涉欲望。其二,顺应万物或百姓的本性。其三,发挥万物或者百姓的自主性。"无为"并不是不作为,而是更智慧的作为方式,通过无为来达到无不为的结果。

Wuwei (non-action) refers to a state of action. Daoism contrasts "action" to "non-action." "Action" generally means that the rulers impose their will on others or the world without showing any respect for or following the intrinsic nature of things. "Non-action" is the opposite of "action," and has three main points: 1) through self-control containing the desire to interfere; 2) following the nature of all things and the people; and 3) bringing into play the initiative of all things and people. "Non-action" does not mean not doing anything, but is a wiser way of doing things. Non-action leads to the result of getting everything done.

引例 Citations:

◎是以圣人处无为之事,行不言之教。(《老子·二章》)

(因此圣人以无为的方式处理世事,以不言的方式教导百姓。)

Therefore sages deal with things through non-action and teach ordinary people through non-speech. (*Laozi*)

◎道常无为而无不为。(《老子·三十七章》)

(道总是对万物不加干涉而成就万物。)

Dao always makes all things possible through non-interference with them. (*Laozi*)

wǔxíng 五行

Wuxing

"五行"有三种不同的含义：其一，指五种最基本的事物或构成万物的五种元素。《尚书·洪范》最早明确了"五行"的内容，即金、木、水、火、土。五种事物或元素有其各自的属性，彼此间存在相生相克的关系。其二，五行进一步被抽象为理解万物和世界的基本框架，万物都可以纳入到五行的范畴之中，并因此被赋予不同的性质。其三，指五种道德行为。荀子（前313？—前238）曾指责子思（前483—前402）、孟子（前372？—前289）"按往旧造说，谓之五行"，从郭店楚墓竹简及马王堆汉墓帛书相关文字内容来看，该"五行"指仁、义、礼、智、圣。

There are three meanings to the term. 1) The five fundamental things or elements that make up all things. *The Book of History* was the first to define the five elements: metal, wood, water, fire, and earth. Each of these has its own properties and they interact in a generative or destructive relationship. 2) On a more abstract level, the term refers to the basic framework to understand the world. All things can be included in the realm of *wuxing* (五行) and their properties are explained or understood accordingly. 3) It refers to five kinds of moral behavior. Xunzi (313?-238 BC) once criticized Zisi (483-402 BC) and Mencius (372?-289 BC) for "creating *wuxing* on the basis of old theories." Ancient bamboo slips unearthed from a grave at Guodian dating back to the State of Chu as well as inscribed silk texts from the Mawangdui Tomb of the Western Han Dynasty, all describe this *wuxing* as benevolence, righteousness, *li* (礼), wisdom, and the wisdom and character of a sage.

引例 Citations：

◎天有三辰，地有五行。(《左传·昭公三十二年》)
（天有日月星三辰，地有金木水火土五行。）

In heaven there are the sun, moon, and stars, while on earth there are the five elements: metal, wood, water, fire, and earth. (*Zuo's Commentary on The Spring and Autumn Annals*)

◎天地之气，合而为一，分为阴阳，判为四时，列为五行。(董仲舒《春秋繁露·五行相生》)
（天地之气，聚合而为一，区别而为阴阳，分判为春夏秋冬四时，排列为金木水火土五行。）

The *qi* of heaven and that of earth merge into one; it evolves into yin and yang, the four seasons, and the five elements of metal, wood, water, fire, and earth. (Dong Zhongshu: *Luxuriant Gems of The Spring and Autumn Annals*)

wù 物

Wu (Thing / Matter)

"物"一般指天地之间有形有象的一切存在，大体有三种不同含义：其一，指有形的具体存在物，包括各种自然物、人造物，也包括各种生物和人。其二，指人伦关系中发生的事务、事情，如侍奉父母、为政治国等，这个意义上的"物"相当于"事"。其三，指具体存在物或人伦事务的总和，通常称"万物"。

Wu (物) usually denotes an existence in the universe that has a form or an image. In general, the word has three different meanings. First, it refers to any concrete existence, encompassing all natural and man-made objects, all organisms and human beings. Second, it covers interpersonal matters and activities such as taking care of one's parents, entering politics, or managing state affairs. In this sense, wu means "matter." Third, the word sums up all existing physical and social matters, generally called "everything."

引例 Citations：

◎有天地，然后万物生焉。盈天地之间者唯万物。(《周易・序卦》)
（先有天地，然后万物化生。充满天地之间的只是万物。）

First, there is the universe. Then everything comes into being and fills up the universe. (*The Book of Changes*)

◎意之所用，必有其物，物即事也。如意用于事亲，即事亲为一物。(《传习录》卷中)
（良知感应运用，必然用于"物"上，"物"就是各种事，如良知感应运用于侍奉双亲，那么侍奉双亲就是一个"物"。）

Conscience must relate to "things," which refer to various matters. If one's conscience is applied to parents, then taking care of one's parents is the "matter." (*Records of Great Learning*)

xiàng wài zhī xiàng, jǐng wài zhī jǐng 象外之象，景外之景

The Image Beyond an Image, the Scene Beyond a Scene

欣赏诗歌的过程中所产生的文本形象之外的第二艺术形象，是读者经联想产生的精神意象。前一个"象""景"指诗歌作品中直接描写的物象和景象，后一个"象""景"则是指由此引发读者多方面联想所营造出的新的意象和意境。由道家与《周易》关于"言"（语言）、"意"（思想或意义）、"象"（象征某种深意的具体形象）三者关系的学说发展而来。魏晋至唐代的诗学倡导"象外之象，景外之景"，旨在追求文本之外的精神蕴涵和意象之美。这一术语同时也表现了中华民族的艺术趣味与审美境界。

Readers of poetry create images and scenes in their minds based on what they are reading. These are the readers' imaginations based on what is depicted in the poems. The term comes from Daoist theories about the relationships between discourses, ideas or meanings, and images that symbolize profound meaning in *The Book of Changes*. From the Wei, Jin to the Tang Dynasty, poetry critics sought "the image beyond an image, the scene beyond a scene" in order to pursue the spiritual implications and the beauty of images that are beyond textual descriptions. This term gives expression to the artistic and aesthetic tastes and ideals of the Chinese nation.

引例 Citations：

◎诗家之景，如蓝田日暖，良玉生烟，可望而不可置于眉睫之前也。象外之象，景外之景，岂容易可谈哉！（司空图《与[汪]极浦书》）
（诗歌所描写的景致，犹如蓝田蕴藏着美玉，玉的烟气在温暖的阳光中若隐若现，可以远远望见，但是不能就近清楚地观察。通过欣赏诗歌景象而产生的之外的景象，岂可容易表达出来呀！）

The imagery of poets is like the sunshine warming Lantian so that fine jades under its ground issue smoke: They can be seen from afar but not observed right before your eyes. The image beyond an image, the scene beyond a scene – are they not simply beyond words! (Sikong Tu: Letter to Wang Jipu)

◎盖诗之所以为诗者，其神在象外，其象在言外，其言在意外。（彭辂《诗集自序》）
（大概诗之所以成为诗，就在于神韵在物象之外，物象在语言之外，语言在意义之外。）

That which makes a poem a poem is a poetic appeal beyond the image, an image beyond the words and words saying things beyond their meaning. (Peng Lu: Preface to *Collected Poems of Peng Lu*)

xiéhé-wànbāng 协和万邦

Coexistence of All in Harmony

指古代有贤德的君主通过实行仁政，将天下诸侯都聚集在自己周围，以实现不同部族、不同国家、不同民族的融合和文化上的涵化，形成和谐统一的部落联盟或多民族国家。这一思想是中国文化整体和谐观的重要表现，是中华民族文化精神的核心观念。

The term refers to the exercise of benevolent government by virtuous and wise rulers in ancient China to win the allegiance of all the vassals, so as to achieve an integration and acculturation of different tribes, nations or ethnic groups and create a harmonious and unified alliance of tribes or a multi-ethnic state. Harmonious coexistence of all is a key feature of the concept of social harmony in Chinese culture and one of the core values of the Chinese nation.

引例 Citation：

◎克明俊德，以亲九族。九族既睦，平（pián）章百姓。百姓昭明，协和万邦，黎民于变时雍。(《尚书·尧典》)
([帝尧]能够明扬大德，使自己的氏族亲善。自己的氏族亲善以后，辨明部落百官族姓的等次。百官族姓的等次明晰之后，大大小小的诸侯国才能和谐共融，普通民众也才能变得和睦。)

(Emperor Yao) was able to promote moral values, so that amity prevailed in his clan. He then clarified the hierarchical order of tribal officials. Only when this was done could all vassal states, big and small, prosper in harmony, and the people become friendly with each other. (*The Book of History*)

xīn 心

Heart / Mind

"心"是人之情感、认识和价值的基础，生命的主宰。与耳、目、鼻、口等被动地感知外物不同,"心"具有思考的能力,可以辨别和整理感官所获得的材料,进行知识和道德判断。孟子(前372?—前289)认为"心"包含恻隐、辞让、羞恶、是非等四端,道德实践的核心就是保存并扩充人固有的善心。道家则认为虚静是心的根本状态,如静止之水,由此可以把握天地万物的本原。

The heart, a vital organ of life, underpins one's emotions, awareness, and value judgments. Different from the ears, eyes, nose, and mouth, which sense the outer world in a passive way, the heart is capable of thinking and performing intellectual and moral evaluations on the basis of analyzing and sorting out what these organs have sensed. Mencius (372?-289 BC) believed that the heart consists of four aspects: compassion, deference, sense of shame or detestation, and conscience. Preserving and expanding one's good heart is the central aim in practicing moral teachings. According to Daoism, a serene and uncluttered heart is the highest state for a human being, much like a peaceful pool of still water. Such calmness is the way in which the heart can capture the essence of all things in the world.

引例 Citations:

◎耳目之官不思,而蔽于物。物交物,则引之而已矣。心之官则思,思则得之,不思则不得也。(《孟子·告子上》)

(耳目等器官不能思考,因而被外物的表象遮蔽。耳目与外物相接触,就会被其引向歧途。"心"这一器官能够思考,思考便能有所得,不思考便无所得。)

The sensory organs like ears and eyes cannot think. Therefore, they tend to be overwhelmed by the representation of external objects, and be led astray by those objects when coming into contact with them. The heart, however, is an organ capable of thinking. Thinking yields insight, while lack of it will get one nowhere. (*Mencius*)

◎心者，一身之主宰。(《朱子语类》卷五)

(心是人身体的主宰。)

Heart is the dominant organ of one's body. (*Classified Conversations of Master Zhu Xi*)

xìn yán bù měi, měi yán bù xìn 信言不美，美言不信

Trustworthy Words May Not Be Fine-sounding; Fine-sounding Words May Not Be Trustworthy.

可信的话并不漂亮，漂亮的话多不可信。老子鉴于当时社会风气与文风的浮华不实，倡导返朴归真与自然平淡的生活方式和文学风格。魏晋时代，文人崇尚自然素朴，反对虚浮华丽的创作风气，出现了像陶渊明（365 或 372 或 376—427）这样伟大的诗人，文艺创作也倡导真实自然的思想与风格。自此之后，中国古代文艺以素朴自然为最高的审美境界。

To address the extravagance in social mores and in the style of writing of his time, Laozi advocated simple and natural lifestyles and literary presentations. During the Wei and Jin dynasties, men of letters valued natural and simple literary styles and were opposed to extravagant and superficial styles. This line of thought led to the emergence of great poets like Tao Yuanming (365 or 372 or 376-427), and shaped literary writings to reflect direct thoughts and natural expressions. Subsequently, ancient Chinese literature and art took simplicity and naturalness as the highest aesthetic standards.

引例 Citations：

◎信言不美，美言不信。善者不辩，辩者不善。(《老子·八十一章》)
（可信的话并不漂亮，漂亮的话多不可信。善良的人往往不能能言善辩，能言善辩的人往往不善良。）

Trustworthy words may not be fine-sounding; fine-sounding words may not be trustworthy. A kind-hearted person may not be an eloquent speaker; a glib person is often not kind. (*Laozi*)

◎老子疾伪，故称"美言不信"，而五千精妙，则非弃美矣。(刘勰《文心雕龙·情采》)
（老子憎恶虚伪矫饰，所以他认为"漂亮的话多不可信"。但他自己写的《道德经》五千言，思想深刻而文笔优美，可见他并没有摒弃文章之美。）

Laozi detested pretense, so he said, "Flowery rhetoric words may not be trustworthy." However, the 5,000-word *Dao De Jing* (another name of *Laozi*) he wrote is not only profound in ideas but reads beautifully. That means he was not opposed to writings using fine words. (Liu Xie: *The Literary Mind and the Carving of Dragons*)

xìng-guān-qún-yuàn 兴观群怨

Stimulation, Contemplation, Communication, and Criticism

孔子（前551—前479）所提出的《诗经》的四种主要功能，实际也是对文学基本功能与价值的高度概括。"兴"是指通过作品的欣赏引发联想，激发欣赏者对于社会人生的思考与志趣提升；"观"是通过作品认识自然与社会人生的各种状况，透视政治得失；"群"是围绕作品与别人展开讨论，交流思想感情；"怨"是表达对社会时政的不满，宣泄内心的情感。这四种功能有着内在的联系，涉及文学的审美功能、认识功能与教育功能。后世学者对此不断有新的阐发。

According to Confucius (551-479 BC), *The Book of Songs* served these four purposes, which summarize the basic functions and values of literature. "Stimulation" means that the appreciation of literary works arouses imagination, stimulates reflection on society and life, and inspires aspirations and interests. "Contemplation" means that reading leads to understanding nature, society, life, and politics. "Communication" means that reading encourages discussion with others, and exchange of thoughts and feelings. "Criticism" means learning how to critically express oneself about state affairs and voice inner feelings. These four functions are closely associated and involve the aesthetic, cognitive, and educational functions of literature. Later scholars have continued to make original contributions to the study of these themes.

引例 Citations：

◎《诗》可以兴，可以观，可以群，可以怨；迩之事父，远之事君；多识于鸟、兽、草、木之名。(《论语·阳货》)
(《诗经》可以感发志向，引发思考，认识世界，可以交流思想感情，表达不满情绪。在家可以用它来侍奉父母，出外可以用它来侍奉国君，还可以从中学到鸟兽草木等众多事物的知识。)

The Book of Songs stimulates the mind, inspires contemplation, enables one to understand society, exchange feelings and thoughts with others, and express resentment. The book guides one on how to support and wait on one's parents at home and how to serve one's sovereign in public life. One can also learn about birds, beasts, and plants from the book. (*The Analects*)

◎于所兴而可观，其兴也深；于所观而可兴，其观也审；以其群者而怨，怨愈不忘；以其怨者而群，群乃益挚。（王夫之《姜斋诗话》卷一）

（经过作者感兴后的作品又具备认识价值，那么这种感兴一定深刻；经过认识又能够激发情感的，那么这种认识一定真实明察；因为聚在一起而产生某种怨恨，那么这种怨恨更加使人难忘；因为某种怨恨而聚成群体，这样的群体一定会更加紧密。）

If works created on the basis of the author's understanding have the value of cognition, his understanding must have been profound. If his feelings are based on recognition, his observation must have been sharp. If certain resentment arises from discussions among a group of people, it must be unforgettable. If a group of people have come together because they share certain resentment, they must be closely knit. (Wang Fuzhi: *Desultory Remarks on Poetry from Ginger Studio*)

xìngxiàng 兴象

Xingxiang (Inspiring Imagery)

文学作品中能够生发深远意旨和审美情境的物象，是创作者主观情感与客观景象完美融合而产生的一种艺术境界。"兴"指作者偶然生发的创作冲动，"象"则是指作者在作品中所借助的外在的具体物象。"兴象"是唐代诗论家殷璠（fán）在《河岳英灵集序》中用来品评盛唐诗人作品的用语，后来演变成诗歌评论的"兴象观"，用以衡量作品境界的高下。

Inspiring imagery is an artistic achievement of profound literary significance and with great aesthetic taste, obtained through the perfect blending of an author's feelings with an objective situation or scenery. *Xing* (兴) is an impromptu inspiration of the author, and *xiang* (象) a material object he borrows from the external world in his writing. Tang-dynasty poetry critic Yin Fan first used the term "inspiring imagery" in his "Preface to *A Collection of Poems by Distinguished Poets*" in commenting on the works of poets in the golden period of the Tang Dynasty. It later became a standard for assessing the merit of a poetic work.

引例 Citations：

◎既多兴象，复备风骨。(殷璠《河岳英灵集》卷三)
(诗人的作品既有许多兴象，又具备了风骨之美。)

These poets' works feature both inspiring imagery, as well as *fenggu* (class and integrity). (Yin Fan: *A Collection of Poems by Distinguished Poets*)

◎作诗大要不过二端：体格声调、兴象风神而已。(胡应麟《诗薮·内编五》)
(作诗大体上有两个方面：体制与声律，兴象与气韵。)

Poetry has two basic aspects: one includes form, rhythm, and rhyme; the other includes imagery and charm. (Hu Yinglin: *An In-depth Exploration of Poetry*)

xìng 性

Xing (Nature)

　　古人所讨论的"性"，主要指"人性"。"性"的概念包含两个要点：其一，是事物天生所具有的属性，非后天人为。其二，是某类事物普遍具有的属性，非某些个体所特有。据此而言，"人性"观念也有两种不同的含义：其一，指人天生所具有的普遍属性，包括身体上的各种生命特征及欲望、知觉等。其二，指人天生所具有的人之所以为人的本质属性，亦即人区别于禽兽的道德本性。历代学者对人性善恶的问题有着许多不同的看法，或性善，或性恶，或性无善恶，或性有善有不善，或有性善有性不善。

Xing (性) mainly referred to human nature in ancient times. The concept of *xing* has two essential points. First, it refers to the inherent nature of all things, not as a result of nurture. Second, it refers to the common nature of certain kind of things, not the nature of individual things of that kind. Similarly, human nature, too, has two meanings. First, it refers to inherent attributes all people share, including physical features, desires, and consciousness. Second, it is the essential and distinct attribute that distinguishes people from birds and beasts, in other words, human's moral nature. Scholars throughout history held varied views over the question whether human nature was good or evil. Some believed it was good. Some thought it was evil. Some held that it was neither good nor evil. Some held that human nature could be both good and evil in the same person. Some thought that human nature was good in some people, but evil in others.

引例 Citations：

◎食、色，性也。(《孟子·告子上》)
（对饮食和美色的追求是人的本性。）

To love food and good looks is but human nature. (*Mencius*)

◎性即理也。(《二程遗书》卷二十二上)
（性就是理。）

Human nature is in line with the principles of heaven. (*Writings of the Cheng Brothers*)

xinglíng 性灵

Xingling (Inner Self)

　　本指相对于客观外物的人的心灵世界，包括性情、才智两个方面。南北朝时期，"性灵"成为文学创作与文学批评术语，主要指与社会伦理、政治教化与传统创作观念相对的个体的精神才智与性情气质，强调文艺应该发自并表现人的性灵。明清时期，随着个性伸张与思想解放，袁宏道（1568—1610）、袁枚（1716—1798）等著名文士用"性灵"倡导文学应该直抒胸臆，表现内心真实的思想情感、兴趣见解，强调创作中的精神个性和艺术个性，反对宋明理学、传统创作观念以及复古思潮对于人性与文学的束缚，并因此成为文学创作上的一个重要流派。

The term refers to an individual's inner mind vis-à-vis the outside world, which consists of two aspects, namely, temperament and talent. During the Southern and Northern Dynasties, *xingling* (inner self) became widely used in literary writing and criticism. It refers to the combination of a writer's temperament and talent, other than his social ethics, political beliefs, and literary traditions; and it stresses that literature is inspired by traits of individuality and should give expression to them. During the Ming and Qing dynasties, along with the trend of giving free rein to individuality and shaking off intellectual straitjacket, renowned scholars such as Yuan Hongdao (1568-1610) and Yuan Mei (1716-1798) advocated giving full expression to one's inner self, namely, one's thoughts, sentiment, emotion and views. They underscored the role of intellectual and artistic individuality in literary creation as opposed to the rigid School of Principle of the earlier Song and Ming dynasties, literary dogma and blind belief in classicism which constrained people from expressing human nature and inhabited literary creativity. The Xingling School thus became an important school in literary creation.

xiū-qí-zhì-píng 修齐治平

Self-cultivation, Family Regulation, State Governance, Bringing Peace to All Under Heaven

"修身""齐家""治国""平天下"的缩写。以个人自身修养为基础逐步向外扩展，先治理好家庭，进而治理好邦国，更进而安抚和治理天下百姓。这是中国古代儒家伦理哲学和政治抱负的一个重要命题，体现了儒家由个人而家而国而天下层层递进的道德政治观。在逐步向外扩展的过程中，个人的德行和修养与不同层面的政治抱负息息相关。

Self-cultivation is the starting point of several steps moving outward. The next step is managing family affairs, followed by governing the state. The final step is moving to provide peace and sound governance to all under heaven. This process is a fundamental theme in Confucian moral philosophy and discourse on politics. It is a gradually expanding process beginning with the individual and emanating outward into serving and benefiting an ever-larger whole. In such a process an individual's virtue and self-improvement are inseparable from his political aspirations.

引例 Citation：

◎古之欲明明德于天下者，先治其国。欲治其国者，先齐其家。欲齐其家者，先修其身。(《礼记·大学》)

（过去想要在全天下彰明光明德性的人，先要治理好自己的邦国。想要治理好自己的邦国，先要治理好自己的家［周朝时为封地］。想要治理好自己的家，先要做好自身的修养。）

The ancients, who wished to promote illustrious virtue under heaven, first had to rule their own states well. Wishing to govern their states well, they first had to manage their fiefdoms well. Wishing to manage their fiefdoms well, they first had to cultivate themselves. (*The Book of Rites*)

xū 虚

Xu (Void)

"虚"指世界或者心灵的一种状态。大体有两种不同的含义：其一，指世界的本原，万物皆由虚无中来。但古人对"虚"的这一含义又有不同理解：或认为"虚"就是空虚无有；或认为"虚"指"气"的存在状态，因为"气"的存在隐微无形，故以"虚"称之，但并非完全空无。其二，指虚静的或没有成见的内心状态。

Xu refers to a state of the cosmos or a state of mind. Basically, it has two different meanings. The first refers to the origin of the universe, indicating that everything originates from *xu*. Different ancient thinkers have different interpretations of this notion: Some take *xu* as being devoid of anything; others believe it is the state of existence of *qi* (气). Because *qi* is invisible and formless, it is said to be empty, but not a vacuum totally devoid of anything. The second meaning of *xu* refers to a state of mind that is peaceful, not preoccupied or simply free of any preconceptions.

引例 Citations：

◎太虚无形，气之本体。（张载《正蒙·太和》）
（太虚是无形的，是气的本来状态。）

Taixu is formless; it is the original state of *qi*. (Zhang Zai: *Enlightenment Through Confucian Teachings*)

◎唯道集虚，虚者心斋也。（《庄子·人间世》）
（道只能集于虚无之气中，虚静的心灵就是"心斋"。）

Dao gathers and presents itself in an unoccupied and peaceful mind; being unoccupied means the pure state of the mind. (*Zhuangzi*)

xūjìng 虚静

Void and Peace

排除一切欲望与理性思维的干扰，达到心灵的纯净与安宁。由道家老庄最先提出，荀子（前313？—前238）也用它说明专心致志所达到的一种精神状态。由于这种心境与文艺审美中无物无我、无知无欲的心理特性相通，因此，古代思想家与文艺批评家也用"虚静"来说明文艺活动中的审美心理。这一术语强调文艺创作中的心灵自由，认为它是达到审美最高境界的重要前提。

Void and peace mean that all distractions, such as desires and rational thoughts, should be dispelled to attain peace and purity of the soul. The idea of void and peace was first proposed by Laozi and Zhuangzi (369?-286 BC), the founders of Daoism, and then used by Xunzi (313?-238 BC) to refer to a state of mental concentration. Such a state of mind is similar to the psychological conditions in appreciation of works of literature and art, which are characterized by being totally free from the awareness of oneself and the outside world, and free from any urge and desire. Therefore, thinkers and literary critics of earlier times used this term to explain the state of mind in literary and artistic creation and appreciation. It stressed the need for spiritual freedom in artistic creation, suggesting that this is an important precondition for reaching the highest level of aesthetic appreciation.

引例 Citations：

◎致虚极，守静笃。(《老子·十六章》)
(达到虚空境界，没有任何杂念；坚守安宁心境，不受外物干扰。)

When one attains the state of void and peace, his mind becomes peaceful and free of any distractions. He can withstand the temptations of the outside world. (*Laozi*)

◎是以陶钧文思，贵在虚静，疏瀹(yuè)五藏(zàng)，澡雪精神。(刘勰《文心雕龙·神思》)
(因此构思文章，最重要的是虚静，不受外物干扰，身体舒泰如同五脏贯通了一样，精神洁净如同洗洁过一样。)

In conceiving an essay, one should strive for a mental state of quiet emptiness and not let oneself be bothered by external interferences, and be relaxed and at ease just like all his internal organs are put in perfect comfort and his spirits refreshed by a thorough wash. (Liu Xie: *The Literary Mind and the Carving of Dragons*)

xuánlǎn 玄览

Xuanlan (Pure-minded Contemplation)

原指在深远虚净的心境下览知万物，是老子提出的认识"道"的一种方法。老子认为，只有摒弃一切杂念与成见，保持内心明澈如镜，才能静观万物，从而认识"道"，体会其精要。后世文艺评论家因为"玄览"所主张的心境与文艺创作及鉴赏所要求的审美心境相契合，遂用为文艺思想的重要术语，以说明文艺创作与鉴赏时应具有的超越一切欲望与功利的特殊心境。

This term was first used by Laozi as a way to understand Dao. He believed that one cannot understand Dao by calmly observing everything unless one abandons all distracting thoughts and biases, and keeps one's mind as clear as a mirror. Later literary critics believed that the state of mind as required for *xuanlan* has similarities with the state of mind required for literary writing and appreciation, thus they made it an important term to mean one's state of mind must transcend all desires and personal gains in literary writing and appreciation.

引例 Citations：

◎涤除玄览，能无疵乎？（《老子·十章》）

（涤除一切杂念，在深远虚静的心境下观照一切，就没有瑕疵了吗？）

Is it for sure that there will be no flaws when one cleanses away all distracting thoughts and watches the world with a clear, peaceful mind? (*Laozi*)

◎伫中区以玄览，颐情志于典坟。（陆机《文赋》）

（久立于天地间以深远虚静的心境观照一切，在典籍的阅读中颐养性情、培养志向。）

Standing between heaven and earth and watching the world with a clear, peaceful mind, the writer enriches and improves himself through reading great works of the past. (Lu Ji: The Art of Writing)

xuǎnjǔ 选举

Select and Recommend

选拔和推举德才兼备的人。自上而下叫做"选"，自下而上叫做"举"。作为官吏选用制度，由国家确定人才选拔的标准，把德才出众的人"选举"到政权体系中来，授以官职，治理国家，以达成理想的统治状态。这种制度，虽因朝代和时势变迁而不尽相同，但大都注重品德、才智及门第出身等条件，基本保障了政权体系和社会精英之间的纵向贯通。它是"人治""德政"理念的体现。

This term refers to the traditional way through which men were selected and appointed to government offices. Designed to achieve an ideal state of rule, the method worked to select and recommend people with outstanding virtue and talent into the system of political power and put them to official posts, where they took charge of the governance of the country. Although the mechanism varied from dynasty to dynasty, it always emphasized a person's moral integrity, ability, wisdom, and family background. It basically ensured that social elites had vertical mobility in the system of political power, and reflected the concepts of "rule by man" and "rule of virtue."

引例 Citation：

◎选举之法，大略有四：曰学校，曰科目，曰荐举，曰铨选。学校以教育之，科目以登进之，荐举以旁招之，铨选以布列之，天下人才尽于是矣。(《明史·选举志一》)

(选举官吏的方法，大体有四种：官学推荐，科举录用，举荐产生，选材授官。官学用来培育人才，科举用来录取人才，举荐作为佐助手段招揽人才，吏部选材授官，使人才遍布各处，天下的人才全都收揽进来了。)

Officials were chosen mainly through four channels: recommendations by government-run schools, imperial civil examinations, recommendations, and selection according to ability. Schools trained talent, imperial civil examinations recruited talent, recommendations served as a supplementary means to seek talent, and the Ministry of Civil Appointment selected officials according to their ability. In this way, all talent in the country could be recruited. (*The History of the Ming Dynasty*)

yǎsú 雅俗

Highbrow and Lowbrow

指文艺作品品味的雅正与通俗、高尚与低俗。是文艺批评中评论作品品味高下的一对范畴。"雅"指作品的品味高雅正统，符合主流的意识形态；"俗"多指流行于大众与民间的世俗审美标准。从文艺创作上说，高雅文艺优美精良，但人工雕琢的痕迹较重；而通俗文艺源自民间，自然清新，质朴粗放。唐以后，不少文人从通俗文艺中汲取养分，通俗文艺逐渐增多，丰富了社会文艺生活，推动了文艺形态的丰富和发展。

Highbrow and lowbrow, a dichotomy in literary criticism, refer to two kinds of literary and artistic works, namely, the refined versus the popular, and the lofty versus the vulgar. Highbrow describes works that are elegant and reflect what conforms with mainstream ideology, whereas lowbrow-art forms tend to meet popular aesthetic standard. From the perspective of art creation, highbrow art may be exquisite, but often appears affected, whereas lowbrow art, which has a folk origin, is natural, refreshing, unaffected, and unconstrained. From the Tang Dynasty onward, it became a trend for men of letters to borrow the best from popular art, thus further spurring the growth of lowbrow art, enriching cultural life and leading to more diversified artistic expressions.

引例 Citations：

◎子曰："恶紫之夺朱也，恶郑声之乱雅乐也，恶利口之覆邦家者。"(《论语·阳货》)

(孔子说："我厌恶用紫色取代红色，厌恶用郑国的音乐扰乱雅正的音乐，憎恶伶牙俐齿而使国家倾覆的人。")

Confucius said, "I detest replacing red with purple and interfering refined classical music with the music of the State of Zheng. I loathe those who overthrow the state with their glib tongues." (*The Analects*)

◎是以绘事图色，文辞尽情，色糅而犬马殊形，情交而雅俗异势。(刘勰《文心雕龙·定势》)

(因此绘画要讲究色彩，写文章要尽力表现思想感情。调配不同的色彩，所画出的狗和马形状才有区别；思想感情有了交错融合，文章的雅俗才显出不同的体势。)

The art of painting requires masterful use of colors, while the art of writing entails effective expression of thoughts and emotions. One needs to blend different colors in order to depict the different shapes of dogs and horses. Only writings that integrate thoughts and emotions demonstrate their highbrow or lowbrow qualities. (Liu Xie: *The Literary Mind and the Carving of Dragons*)

yǎngqì 养气

Cultivate *Qi*

涵养道德精神、调养身心健康以达到良好的心态，从而创作出优秀的文艺作品。这一术语具有多重蕴涵：其一，先秦孟子（前372？—前289）强调君子应善于培养道德精神的"浩然之气"。其二，东汉王充（27—97？）在《论衡》中有《养气篇》，专门从养生角度提倡"养气"。其三，南朝刘勰（465？—520）《文心雕龙·养气》，汲取上述思想，主张在从事文艺创作的初始阶段，要保持良好的身体状态和从容自由的心态，不应过度消耗精神。后来"养气"成为文艺心理学的重要术语。

This term suggests cultivating one's moral spirit and improving one's physical and mental well-being to achieve the best state of mind in order to write excellent works. "Cultivating *qi* (气)" has three implications: 1) in the pre-Qin period Mencius (372?-289 BC) emphasized that the virtuous and the capable should foster a "noble spirit" conducive to moral cultivation; 2) *A Comparative Study of Different Schools of Learning* by Wang Chong (27-97?) of the Eastern Han Dynasty has a chapter entitled "Treatise on Cultivating *Qi*," which emphasizes *qi* cultivation primarily in regards to maintaining good health; 3) Liu Xie (465?-520) of the Southern Dynasties, in *The Literary Mind and the Carving of Dragons*, drew upon the foregoing ideas and suggested maintaining good physical condition and a free, composed mental state in the initial phase of literary creation, while opposing excessive mental exertion. "Cultivating *qi*" subsequently became an important term in the lexicon of literary psychology.

引例 Citations：

◎我知言，我善养吾浩然之气。(《孟子·公孙丑上》)
(我能够识别各种言论中的思想感情倾向，这是因为我懂得如何培养自己正大刚强的"气"。)

I am capable of differentiating between the thoughts and sentiments people convey in their words because I know how to cultivate my *qi*, and keep it strong. (*Mencius*)

◎是以吐纳文艺，务在节宣，清和其心，调畅其气；烦而即舍，勿使壅滞。(刘勰《文心雕龙·养气》)
(因此从事写作必须学会节制和疏导，让内心纯净平和，将气调理顺畅，内心烦乱时就应停止，不要让思路滞涩。)

Hence, when engaging in writing one must learn how to constrain and regulate oneself, keep one's mind pure and peaceful, and modulate one's mental vitality and activities. One should stop writing when upset so as not to disrupt one's train of thinking. (Liu Xie: *The Literary Mind and the Carving of Dragons*)

yī 一

The One

"一"有三种不同含义：其一，指万物的本体或本原，即"道"的别称，或称"太一"。其二，指天地未分之时的混沌状态。"一"分化形成天地，天地万物都产生于这样一个混沌的统一体。其三，指事物的统一性，与"多""两"相对，意在强调有差异或对立的事物之间的统一性。

The term has three meanings. First, it indicates the original essence of all things. It is another name for *dao* (way). It is also referred to as *taiyi* (the supreme one). Second, it refers to the state of chaos before the separation of heaven and earth. The one was divided and transformed into heaven and earth. All things in heaven and on earth were produced from this chaotic entity. Third, it indicates the unity of things, as opposed to "many" or "two." The idea is to emphasize the unity among things which are different or opposite.

引例 Citations：

◎一者，万物之所从始也。（董仲舒《举贤良对策》）
（"一"是万物产生的端始。）

The one is the origin of everything. (Dong Zhongshu: *Replies to the Emperor's Questions After Being Recommended*)

◎两不立则一不可见，一不可见则两之用息。（张载《正蒙·太和》）
（没有相反两方的对立则统一体不可得见，统一体不可得见则相反两方的对立也就消失了。）

Unity cannot be seen without the contradiction between two opposite sides, while the two opposite sides cannot exist without unity. (Zhang Zai: *Enlightenment Through Confucian Teachings*)

yì 义

Righteousness

"义"的基本含义是合理、恰当，引申而有两重含义：其一，指人行事的合理依据与标准。其二，指在道德意识的判断与引导下，调节言行使之符合一定的标准，以获得合理的安处。宋代学者用"理"或"天理"的概念来解释"义"，认为"义"就是"天理"所规定的合理的标准，同时要求言行符合"天理"。

The basic meaning of *yi* (义) is "reasonable" and "proper." It has two extended meanings. One is the proper basis and standard for people's actions. The other is to adjust one's words or deeds to meet certain standards, under the guidance of moral judgments. Scholars in the Song Dynasty used *li* (理) or "principles of heaven" to interpret *yi*, and considered *yi* to be the reasonable standard defined by the "principles of heaven," and hoped that people's words and deeds would fall in line with the "principles of heaven."

引例 Citations：

◎君子喻于义。(《论语·里仁》)
(君子知晓并遵循义。)

A man of virtue understands and does what is morally right. (*The Analects*)

◎义者，心之制，事之宜也。(朱熹《孟子集注》卷一)
(义就是约束自己的内心，使事情合宜。)

Righteousness means exercising self-restraint in order to do everything properly. (Zhu Xi: *Mencius Variorum*)

yìxiàng 意象

Yixiang (Imagery)

文学作品中表达作者主观情感和独特意境的典型物象。"意"指作者的思想情感;"象"是外在的具体物象,是寄寓了作者思想情感的艺术形象。在文学创作中,"意象"多指取自大自然中能够寄托情思的物象。"意象"强调文学作品的思想内容与形象之美的和谐生成,是一种成熟的文艺形态。

Imagery refers to a typical image in literary works, which embodies the author's subjective feelings and unique artistic conceptions. *Yi* (意) literally means an author's feelings and thoughts, and *xiang* (象) refers to the image of a material object in the external world, an artistic image reflecting the author's thoughts and feelings. In literary creation, imagery often refers to those images in nature with which an author's feelings and thoughts are associated. Emphasizing the harmonious relationship between beauty in both form and content, it is a mature state of literary creation.

引例 Citations:

◎窥意象而运斤。(刘勰《文心雕龙·神思》)

(探寻心中的意象而构思运笔。)

An author explores the imagery in his mind, conceives a work, and writes it down. (Liu Xie: *The Literary Mind and the Carving of Dragons*)

◎意象欲出,造化已奇。(司空图《二十四诗品·缜密》)

(诗歌的意象浑欲浮现,大自然是这般奇妙。)

What a wonderful state of nature it is when the imagery of a poem is about to emerge! (Sikong Tu: Twenty-four Styles of Poetry)

yīnyáng 阴阳

Yin and Yang

  本义指物体对于日光的向背，向日为"阳"，背日为"阴"。引申而有两重含义：其一，指天地之间性质相反的两种气。其二，指两种最基本的矛盾势力或属性，凡动的、热的、在上的、向外的、明亮的、亢进的、强壮的为"阳"，凡静的、寒的、在下的、向内的、晦暗的、减退的、虚弱的为"阴"。"阴""阳"或"阴气""阳气"的相互作用决定着万物的生成及存在状态。阴阳理论后来成为古人说明和理解宇宙万物、社会和人伦秩序的基础，如天阳地阴、君阳臣阴、夫阳妻阴等，阳贵阴贱，阳主阴从。

The primary meaning of yin and yang is the orientation of things in relation to the sun, with yang meaning the sunny side and yin the shady side. There are two extended meanings: 1) two opposite kinds of *qi* (气) in nature; and 2) two basic contrary forces or qualities that coexist, thus the active, hot, upward, outward, bright, forward, and strong are yang, while the passive, cold, downward, inward, dark, backward, and weak are yin. The interaction between yin and yang, or yin *qi* and yang *qi*, determines the formation and existence of all things. The theory of yin and yang later became the basis for ancient Chinese to explain and understand the universe and everything in it, social order, and human relations. For example, heaven is yang and earth is yin, ruler is yang and subordinates are yin, husband is yang and wife is yin, noble is yang and ignoble is yin, leading is yang and following is yin.

引例 Citations：

◎万物负阴而抱阳，冲气以为和。(《老子·四十二章》)

（万物背阴而向阳，阴阳两气互相激荡而成调和状态。）

All things stand, facing yang and against yin. The interaction between yin and yang creates a state of harmony. (*Laozi*)

◎阴阳无所独行。(董仲舒《春秋繁露·基义》)

（阴与阳不能单独发生作用。）

Yin and yang cannot work without each other. (Dong Zhongshu: *Luxuriant Gems of The Spring and Autumn Annals*)

yǐnxiù 隐秀

Latent Sentiment and Evident Beauty

　　诗歌与文章既隐含丰富的思想感情，又有秀美的名言佳句。出自《文心雕龙》篇名。"隐"是隐含，指在叙事或写景中隐含超出事、景之外的意义，能引发读者的无限联想；"秀"是秀美，指一篇之中应该有能凸显这一意义的精妙词句。二者密不可分，共同构成优秀文学作品的审美特征。后来也作为诗文写作的一种修辞手法。

This term means that prose and poetry may contain latent sentiments and thoughts, as well as expressions and sentences that present an apparent sense of beauty. "Latent sentiment and evident beauty" first appeared as the title of a chapter in *The Literary Mind and the Carving of Dragons*. There, "latent sentiment" means what lies beyond events and landscapes in a narrative or a description, triggering imaginations on the part of the reader. On the other hand, "evident beauty" refers to the kind of beauty created by expressions and sentences in a piece of writing, which bring out that latent meaning. The latent and the apparent qualities are inseparable, constituting an aesthetic feature of good literary works. Later, this term developed into a rhetorical device in writing prose and poetry.

引例 Citations：

◎是以文之英蕤，有秀有隐。隐也者，文外之重旨者也；秀也者，篇中之独拔者也。(刘勰《文心雕龙·隐秀》)
(因此优秀的文章要兼具"秀"和"隐"。所谓"隐"，就是指文章在语言之外隐含有多重意蕴；所谓"秀"，则是有既彰显主旨又独到突出的秀美词句。)

Thus, an excellent piece of writing should have both beautiful in language and a message hidden between the lines. The former refers to beautiful sentences and expressions that accentuate the message of the writing while the latter represents the multiple significance that lies beyond the text. (Liu Xie: *The Literary Mind and the Carving of Dragons*)

◎情在词外曰隐，状溢目前曰秀。(张戒《岁寒堂诗话》卷上引刘勰语)
(思想感情隐含于语言背后叫做"隐"，寄寓思想感情的景象鲜活地展现在读者眼前叫做"秀"。)

Latency happens when feelings and thoughts are hidden between the lines of a literary work. Evident beauty occurs when messages of sentiment and feelings are vividly portrayed by the images the author creates. (Zhang Jie: *Notes on Poetry Written in the Pine and Cypress Studio*)

yǒu dé zhě bì yǒu yán 有德者必有言

Virtuous People Are Sure to Produce Fine Writing.

品德高尚的人一定有著述或妙文传世。儒家认为作家的人品（道德修养）与作品（文章价值）往往有内在的联系，品德高尚的人文章自然高妙，而善写文章的人却未必道德高尚，以此提出作家著述应以传播道德为使命，道德文章要相互统一。但后世儒家文士有时过于强调文章的道德作用与作家个人品德对文章的影响从而忽视了文学自身的创作特点与价值。

Virtuous people are sure to write fine works which will be passed on to later generations. According to Confucianism, the moral character of a writer determines the value of his work, virtuous people would naturally write well, but those who wrote well might not necessarily be virtuous. Therefore, authors should write to disseminate moral values; virtue and writings should be consistent. However, later Confucian scholars sometimes overemphasized the influence that ethics and the authors' moral character had on their writings to the neglect of the characteristics and values of literary creation per se.

引例 Citations：

◎子曰："有德者必有言，有言者不必有德。"（《论语·宪问》）
（孔子说："道德高尚的人，一定有名言传世；有名言传世的人，不一定道德高尚。"）

Confucius said, "Virtuous people are sure to have good writings or words to pass on to later generations, but it is not always true the other way round." (*The Analects*)

◎丈夫处世，怀宝挺秀。辨雕万物，智周宇宙。立德何隐，含道必授。（刘勰《文心雕龙·诸子》）

（大丈夫活在世上，应该身怀才能，超群出众，雄辩的文辞可以摹写万物，周全的智慧可以穷尽宇宙奥秘。何须隐藏自己立德的志向，掌握了道就一定要广泛传授。）

A man of character should possess exceptional capability and his eloquent expressions should portray everything truthfully. His great wisdom should enable him to explain all things under heaven. He does not need to hide his aspirations to serve as a model of virtue. If he has come to a good understanding of Dao, he surely will disseminate it extensively. (Liu Xie: *The Literary Mind and the Carving of Dragons*)

yǒujiào-wúlèi 有教无类

Education for All Without Discrimination

任何人都可以或必须接受教化；而人接受了教化，也就没有了因贵贱、贫富等而产生的差异。（一说：在教学时对学生一视同仁，不会按地位、贫富等将学生分成差等。）"教"指礼乐教化，即"人文"；"类"即种类，指贵贱、贫富、智愚、善恶、地域、种族等差别、区分。"有教无类"所昭示的是一种超越等级、地域、种族等差别的普及教育思想，更是一种主张平等待人、反对种种歧视的"人文"精神。

Education can and must be provided for all. It eliminates the differences in social status and wealth. (Another explanation is that education should be provided to students without discrimination on the basis of social status or wealth.)

Education consists of teaching of social norms, music, and moral principles. A non-discriminatory approach to education means making no distinction between students based on their social status, wealth, mental capability, moral character, geographic location, or ethnicity. Transcending differences in social status, geography, and ethnicity, education for all without discrimination is a humanistic ideal that champions equal treatment of all people and rejects all forms of discrimination.

引例 Citation：

◎圣人之道无不通，故曰"有教无类"。彼创残之余，以穷归我。我援护之，收处内地，将教以礼法，职以耕农……何患之恤？（《新唐书·突厥传上》）（圣人的道德教化无处不相通，所以说"只要接受了统一的教化，就不会再有因地域、种族产生的差异"。他们突厥人遭受战争创伤，因处困境而归顺于大唐。我们帮助、保护他们，把他们迁入内地定居，教他们礼仪法度，使他们以耕田务农为业……有什么可忧虑的呢？）

The moral values promoted by ancient sages are universal. That is why "once the same education is provided, differences in geography and ethnicity would be smoothed out." When the Tujue people who suffered from war trauma and were in predicament submitted themselves to the Tang Dynasty, we should assist and protect them, let them settle down among us, teach them social norms and law, and help them engage in farming… What should we be worried about? (*The New Tang History*)

yǒuwú 有无

You* and *Wu

"有无"有三种不同含义：其一，指个体事物的不同部分，实有的部分为"有"，空虚的部分为"无"。其二，指个体事物在生成、存在、消亡过程中的不同阶段或状态，既有之后、未消亡之前的状态为"有"，未有之前与既终之后的状态为"无"。其三，有形、有名的具体事物或其总和为"有"，超越一切个体事物的无形、无名的本体或本原为"无"。就第三个意义而言，有些哲学家认为"无"是世界的本体或本原，"有"生于"无"；另一些哲学家则认为"有"才是更根本的，反对"有"生于"无"。在"有无"对待的关系中，"有"与"无"既相互区别，又相互依赖。

The term has three definitions. First, it describes two different dimensions of things: One is with form and the other without form. Second, it refers to two different stages or states of a thing during its generation, existence, and demise. *You* (有) refers to the state of a thing after it has come into being and before it dies out; *wu* (无) refers to the state of a thing before its birth and after its death. Third, *you* refers to any tangible or identifiable thing or the sum total of such things; *wu* refers to the original source or ontological existence, which is intangible and unidentifiable, and transcends all specific objects. With regard to the third definition, some philosophers consider *wu* to be the original source or ontological existence of the world, and *you* comes from *wu*; others believe that *you* is fundamentally significant, and dispute the notion that *you* owes its existence to *wu*. Despite their differences, *you* and *wu* are mutually dependent.

引例 Citations:

◎故有之以为利，无之以为用。(《老子·十一章》)
(所以说事物"有"的部分带给人便利，"无"的部分发挥了事物的作用。)

Therefore, the with-form part of an object provides ease and convenience, whereas the without-form part performs the functions of that object. (*Laozi*)

◎有之所始，以无为本。(王弼《老子注》)
("有"之所以肇始存在，以"无"为根本。)

The formation and existence of *you* originate from *wu*. (Wang Bi: *Annotations on Laozi*)

yuánqǐ 缘起

Dependent Origination

梵文 pratītyasamutpāda 的意译。"缘起"就是"依缘（一定的条件）而起（发生）"。意思是一切事物、现象乃至社会的一切活动都是因缘和合体，都处于相续不断的因缘关系中，依一定条件而有生灭变化。"缘起"是佛教思想的起点，也是佛教各宗派所共有的理论基础。佛教以此解释宇宙万物、社会乃至各种精神现象变化无常、生灭变化的内在法则。

The term is a translation of the Sanskrit word *pratītyasamutpāda*. *Yuan* (缘) means conditions; *qi* (起) means origination. That is to say, all things, phenomena, and social activities arise out of the combinations of causes and conditions. They exist in the continuous relationship between causes and conditions. Thus all things originate, change, and demise depending upon certain conditions. Dependent origination is the fountainhead of Buddhist thought and forms the common theoretical basis for all Buddhist schools and sects. Buddhism uses this concept to explain everything in the universe, the constant changes of social and spiritual phenomena, and the internal laws of origination, change, and demise.

引例 Citation：

◎物从因缘故不有，缘起故不无。(僧肇《肇论·不真空论》引《中观》)
(万物依因缘的聚合而成，故不能说"有"；又依一定的缘而有生灭变化，故不能说"无"。)

All things originate out of the combinations of causes and conditions, thus they cannot be regarded as original existence; at the same time, they arise, change, and demise upon certain conditions, so they cannot be said as non-existence. (*Fundamental Verses on the Middle Way*, as cited in Seng Zhao: *Treatise of Seng Zhao*)

zhīyīn 知音

Resonance and Empathy

体会和理解文艺作品的意蕴与作者的思想感情。原指音乐欣赏中的知己，后经魏晋南北朝时期文艺批评家的阐释，用来泛指文艺鉴赏中的心心相印、互相理解。"知音"作为文学批评的核心概念，涉及文艺创作与鉴赏中的个体差异与共性等诸多问题，有着丰富的精神蕴涵，与西方的读者反应批评理论、接受美学、解释学等基本思想有一致之处。

The term is about appreciating and understanding the ideas in literary and artistic works and the thoughts of their authors. The original meaning was feeling a sense of resonance with music. It was later extended by literary critics in the Wei, Jin, and Southern and Northern dynasties to mean resonance or empathy between writers / artists and their readers / viewers. As a core concept in literary criticism, it touches upon both general and particular issues in artistic creation and appreciation, involves rich intellectual implications, and meshes with the audience's response in Western criticism, receptive aesthetics, and hermeneutics.

引例 Citations：

◎是故不知声者不可与言音，不知音者不可与言乐，知乐则几于礼矣。（《礼记·乐记》）

（不懂自然声音的人无法与其谈论音律，不懂音律的人无法与其谈论音乐，通晓音乐的人也就接近懂得礼了。）

Talking about melody with someone who has no ear for natural sounds would be a waste of time, and so would discussing music with someone who knows nothing about melody. One who knows music is close to understanding social norms. (*The Book of Rites*)

◎知音其难哉！音实难知，知实难逢，逢其知音，千载其一乎！（刘勰《文心雕龙·知音》）

（理解音乐是多么困难啊！音乐实在难于理解，理解音乐的人很难遇到，要遇到理解音乐的人，恐怕是千年一遇呀！）

It is such a challenge to understand music! Since music is so hard to understand, it is difficult to find people who can appreciate it. It may take a thousand years to find someone who understands music! (Liu Xie: *The Literary Mind and the Carving of Dragons*)

zhíxún 直寻

Direct Quest

诗人即兴而感，直接抒写。这是南朝钟嵘（？—518？）《诗品》中针对诗歌过多使用典故的现象提出的创作主张，他汲取了道家的自然思想，通过考察前人的优秀诗篇，提炼出一种新的诗歌创作方式——"直寻"，即直接描写所感知事物，直接抒发内心情感并创造出情景契合的审美意象。明清时期诗学的"性灵说"受到其影响。

A poet should directly express his thoughts and sentiments when he is inspired. This is a concept for writing poems proposed by poetry critic Zhong Rong (?-518?) of the Southern Dynasties in his work *The Critique of Poetry* as a reaction to the excessive use of allusions and quotes from earlier works. Inspired by naturalist ideas of Daoism and by his own reading of the fine works of earlier poets, he developed a new form of poetic creation which he named "direct quest." By this, he meant directly describing matters that one senses and learns about, directly expressing one's inner feelings, and creating aesthetic images in which the sensibilities match up with current realities. The theory of inner self used in Ming- and Qing-dynasty poetics was influenced by this idea.

引例 Citations：

◎观古今胜语，多非补假，皆由直寻。（钟嵘《诗品》卷中）

（综观古今名篇佳句，大都不是借用前人诗句或使用典故，而是直接从自身体验中寻求而得。）

A comprehensive survey of the best-known works of ancient and current poets shows that most of the poets did not borrow favored lines or literary allusions from their predecessors, but directly sought inspirations from their personal experiences. (Zhong Rong: *The Critique of Poetry*)

◎我手写我口，古岂能拘牵？（黄遵宪《杂感》其二）

（我要用我的文字来表达我想说的意思，怎么能够为古人文章的思想内容和文字形式所束缚？）

Since I want to use my own words to express my feelings, how can I let myself be bound by the content and forms of ancient writings? (Huang Zunxian: Five Poems on Random Thoughts)

zhōngguó 中国

Zhongguo (China)

　　古代华夏族、汉民族以黄河中下游流域为中心生活和活动的区域。"中国"最初是一个地域兼文化的概念。华夏族多建国于黄河流域一带，以为居天下之中，故称"中国"（与"四方"相对）。后泛指中原地区以及在中原地区建立的政权和国家。清以来，"中国"始专指我国的全部领土与主权，现在只作为"中华人民共和国"的简称。

This term refers to the areas along the middle and lower reaches of the Yellow River where ancient Huaxia (华夏) people or the Han people lived. Originally, the term Zhongguo (中国) meant both this region and its culture. The Huaxia people established their states along the Yellow River. Believing the areas were located in the center of the world, they called it Zhongguo (the Central Country, as against other areas around it). Later, the term was used to refer to the Central Plains in North China and the states founded in that area. Since the Qing Dynasty, Zhongguo has been used to refer specifically to all the territory of China and its sovereignty. Currently, Zhongguo is used as the abbreviated form of the People's Republic of China.

引例 Citations：

◎惠此中国，以绥四方。(《诗经·大雅·民劳》)
（爱护京师百姓，安抚四方诸侯。）

Give benefit to the people in the capital, and reassure and pacify all the feudal dukes and princes in the country. (*The Book of Songs*)

◎若能以吴越之众与中国抗衡，不如早与之绝。(《三国志·蜀书·诸葛亮传》)
（如果能够以江东的兵力与中原抗衡，不如早与他们断绝交往。）

If the areas of Wu and Yue (under the control of Sun Quan) could stand up to confront the central region (under the control of Cao Cao), the former should better cut ties with the latter. (*The History of the Three Kingdoms*)

zhōnghuá 中华

Zhonghua

"中华"是"中国"与"华夏"复合的简称。"华"同"花"，喻指文化灿烂。华夏的先民建国于黄河中下游，自认为居天下之中央，且又文化发达，所以称"中华"。随着华夏族为主体的多民族国家的不断扩张，凡所统辖之地，皆称中华。在近现代历史中，"中华"成为指称中国、中国人及中国文化的一种符号。

This term is an abbreviation of the compound word formed by Zhongguo (中国) and Huaxia (华夏). Here, *hua* (华) also means "flower" or "flowery," which was used as an analogy for a splendid culture. The ancestors of the Huaxia people established their state in the middle and lower reaches of the Yellow River, which they thought was the center (*zhong*) of the world and which had a flourishing culture (*hua*), so the state was called Zhonghua. This multi-ethnic state, with the Huaxia people as the predominant group of its population, later began its territorial expansions, and the places where it extended to became part of Zhonghua. In modern times, Zhonghua became a term denoting China, the Chinese people, and its culture.

引例 Citation：

◎中华者，中国也。亲被王教，自属中国，衣冠威仪，习俗孝悌，居身礼义，故谓之中华。(王元亮《唐律释文》卷三)

(中华即中国。自身接受了王道教化，自然就属于中国了，穿衣戴帽有威仪，风俗讲究孝悌，立身处世追求礼义，所以称之为"中华"。)

Zhonghua refers to China. Under the wise rule of the sage king, all his subjects belong to China. They are dressed in a dignified manner, practice filial piety and fraternal duty, and follow moral norms in personal and social conduct. This is the country called Zhonghua. (Wang Yuanliang: *Commentary and Explanation on Well-Known Law Cases of the Tang Dynasty*)

zhōngyōng 中庸

Zhongyong (Golden Mean)

孔子（前551—前479）和儒家所肯定的最高德行。"中"指言行没有过或不及的状态或标准。凡事都有某种限度，超过和达不到这个限度都是不好的。"庸"包含两个相关的含义：其一指平常，其二指恒常。"中"只有在平常日用之中才能恒常不易。"中庸"即指在人伦日用中始终遵循、符合无过无不及的标准。

Zhongyong (golden mean) was considered to be the highest level of virtue by Confucius (551-479 BC) and Confucian scholars. Zhong (中) means moderate in one's words and deeds. Everything has its limits, and neither exceeding nor falling short of the limits is desirable. Yong (庸) has two meanings. One is common or ordinary and the other is unchanging. Moderation can be maintained for over a long time constantly only when one practices it in everyday life. Zhongyong means the standard of moderation that one should follow in dealing with others and in one's everyday conduct.

引例 Citations：

◎中庸之为德也，其至矣乎！（《论语·雍也》）
（中庸作为一种道德，是最高的准则吧！）

Zhongyong is the highest of virtues. (The Analects)

◎中庸者，不偏不倚、无过不及而平常之理。（朱熹《中庸章句》）
（中庸就是不偏颇，没有过或不及的平常的道理。）

Zhongyong does not bend one way or the other; it is the common principle of neither exceeding nor falling short of the line. (Zhu Xi: *Annotations on The Doctrine of the Mean*)

zīwèi 滋味

Nuanced Flavor

诗歌中能够使欣赏者反复回味的意蕴，实即诗歌美感。南朝诗论家钟嵘（？—518？）在《诗品》中提出，五言诗歌创作应重视内容与形式的配合，使欣赏者在品读中产生无穷的回味。后来"滋味"也指从事文艺创作时的一种趣味。

This term refers to an effect that allows lasting satisfaction and rewarding in poetry appreciation, which is a particular sense of beauty offered by poetry. In the Southern Dynasties, poetry critic Zhong Rong (?-518?) proposed in *The Critique of Poetry* that in writing five-character-per-line poems, one should pay special attention to the combination of form and content, so that readers could enjoy a poem with inexhaustible delight. Later, nuanced flavor also came to refer to a kind of taste in literary and artistic creation.

引例 Citations：

◎五言居文词之要，是众作之有滋味者也。（钟嵘《诗品》卷上）

（五言诗在各种诗体中居于首位，是众多作品中最有审美意味的。）

Five-character-per-line poems constitute the most important poetic form and are most richly imbued with nuanced flavors. (Zhong Rong: *The Critique of Poetry*)

◎至于陶冶性灵，从容讽谏，入其滋味，亦乐事也。（颜之推《颜氏家训·文章》）

（至于文章可以陶冶心灵，从容巧妙地讽谏帝王，使读者感受到一种审美意味。这也是一大快事。）

A literary work cultivates the mind, implicitly satirizes or criticizes a monarch, and enables the reader to obtain a sense of aesthetic appreciation. Reading such works gives one great delight. (Yan Zhitui: *Admonitions for the Yan Clan*)

zǐzhīduózhū 紫之夺朱

Purple Prevailing over Red

指社会生活与文学艺术等领域以邪乱正、真伪混淆的现象。朱指红色，古人认为是正色，而紫色则看作杂色，"夺"是胜过的意思。孔子（前551—前479）对于在春秋时期出现邪正不分、淫靡的音乐取代雅正音乐的现象十分反感，提出要加以正本清源、拨乱反正。南朝刘勰（465？—520）借此批评有的作者在文章写作上背离了儒家经典，迎合人们的猎奇心理。后世以此倡导、确立儒家的文学标准与规范。

This refers to evil prevailing over good and falsehood being mistaken for truth in literature and art as well as in social life. It is red, not purple, that was viewed as a truly proper color by the ancient Chinese. Confucius (551-479 BC), upset by the loss of judgment over good and evil, and by the fact that vulgar music was taking the place of refined classical music in the Spring and Autumn Period, called for dispelling confusion and putting things in the right order. With this in mind, Liu Xie (465?-520) of the Southern Dynasties criticized some writers for abandoning Confucian teachings and catering to vulgar tastes. Scholars of later generations used this notion to reaffirm Confucian criteria and norms for literary creation.

引例 Citations：

◎子曰："恶紫之夺朱也，恶郑声之乱雅乐也，恶利口之覆邦家者。"(《论语·阳货》)

(孔子说："我厌恶用紫色取代红色，厌恶用郑国的音乐扰乱雅正的音乐，憎恶伶牙俐齿而使国家倾覆的人。")

Confucius said, "I detest replacing red with purple and interfering refined classical music with the music of the State of Zheng. I loathe those who overthrow the state with their glib tongues." (*The Analects*)

◎辞为肌肤，志实骨髓。雅丽黼黻，淫巧朱紫。(刘勰《文心雕龙·体性》)

(文辞好比文章的肌肤，作者的思想感情才是文章的骨髓。高雅的文章犹如上古礼服所绣的花纹那样华丽庄重，过分追求辞藻与技巧则如同杂色搅乱了正色。)

Rhetoric is like the skin of an essay; the writer's thoughts and feelings are its marrow. A piece of elegant writing is like the embroidery on a ceremonial gown in ancient times – magnificent and dignified. Excessive focus on rhetoric and technique, however, is no different from an abnormal color taking the place of a truly proper one. (Liu Xie: *The Literary Mind and the Carving of Dragons*)

zìrán 自然

Naturalness

事物的本来状态，旨在与"人为"的意义相区别。哲学意义上的"自然"概念，与常识性的"自然界"概念不同。在日常语义中，"自然界"指人与社会之外的物质世界，这一领域是不受人为干扰的。但从哲学层面来看，人与社会也有其"自然"状态。在政治哲学领域，"自然"特指百姓在不受行政教化干预的情况下自己而然的状态。道家主张，君主治理国家应遵循、顺应百姓的"自然"状态。

The term refers to the primordial state of things, unaffected by the various meanings imposed on it by man. The concept of naturalness in philosophy is different from that of nature in the ordinary sense. In daily language, the term refers to the physical world, which is independent of human interference, as opposed to human society. In philosophy, there is also a natural state of man and society. In political philosophy, "naturalness" specifically applies to the natural state enjoyed by ordinary people free from the intervention of government supervision and moral edification. Daoism holds that in governance a monarch should conform to the natural state of the people.

引例 Citations：

◎道法自然。(《老子·二十五章》)
(道效法万物之自然。)

Dao patterns itself on what is natural. (*Laozi*)

◎天地任自然，无为无造，万物自相治理。(王弼《老子注》)

（天地听任万物之自然，不施为造作，而让万物自己相互治理。）

Heaven and earth allow everything to follow their natural course without imposing any interference so that all things interact and govern themselves. (Wang Bi: *Annotations on Laozi*)

zìrán-yīngzhǐ 自然英旨

Charm of Spontaneity

在诗歌创作中不假雕饰地呈现自然万物之美和人的真情实感。"英旨"本义是美好的滋味，用为文学术语，指诗歌美妙的内容和意境。南朝钟嵘（？—518？）在《诗品》中，要求诗人用自己的语言直接抒写思想感情，反对借用前人的诗句来吟咏自己的情志，批评五言诗创作中过度讲究辞藻和声律，认为符合"自然英旨"的创作才是最为珍贵的诗歌作品。后世文论中的"自然""天真"等词传承了上述内涵。

This term means poetry creation should present the unembellished beauty of nature and the genuine sentiments of human beings. The original meaning of *yingzhi* (英旨) is good taste. Used as a literary term, however, it refers to charming content and aesthetic conception in poetry. In *The Critique of Poetry*, Zhong Rong (?-518?) of the Southern Dynasties called on poets to express their thoughts and sentiments in their own words and opposed borrowing expressions from ancient poets. He criticized the excessive attention to ornate language and tonal rhythms in the writing of five-character-per-line poetry. He maintained that spontaneously created poems of good taste were most valuable. The expressions "natural" and "simple and unaffected" in later literary criticisms contain Zhong Rong's ideas.

引例 Citations：

◎近任昉、王元长等，词不贵奇，竞须新事，尔来作者，寖（jìn）以成俗。遂乃句无虚语，语无虚字；拘挛补衲，蠹文已甚。但自然英旨，罕值其人。（钟嵘《诗品》卷中）

（近来的文人任昉、王融等，不注重语言创新，争相使用各种无人用过的典故，此后的作者逐渐形成了这样的习惯。于是没有不用典故的句子，没有无来历的字词；典故与自己的文字勉强牵合拼贴，对作品破坏严重。几乎很少有诗人能够写出不假雕饰地呈现自然美和真情实感的作品。）

Ren Fang, Wang Rong and some other writers of recent times have given no attention to linguistic innovation yet vied with each other for using literary allusions that no one else has ever employed. Subsequent writers have turned this practice into a habit. And so, all sentences must contain allusions, and every word and expression has to be traceable to some sources. Allusions are clumsily tacked onto the authors' own words, severely damaging their works. There are few poets capable of producing works that display the pristine beauty of nature or their genuine sentiments. (Zhong Rong: *The Critique of Poetry*)

◎所示书教及诗赋杂文，观之熟矣。大略如行云流水，初无定质，但常行于所当行，常止于所不可不止，文理自然，姿态横生。（苏轼《答谢民师书》）

（你给我看的信和诗赋杂文，我阅读得很熟了。大致都像飘动着的云和流动着的水一样，本来没有固定的形态，经常行进在应当行进的地方，经常停止于不得不停止的地方，文章条理自然，姿态多变而不受拘束。）

I have read with great interest the letters, poems, and essays you have sent to me. Broadly speaking, they are all like floating clouds and flowing waters, have no set form or structure, and frequently move when they should move and remain still when they must stop. The articles are presented in a natural way and have multiple and uninhibited styles. (Su Shi: A Letter of Reply to Xie Minshi)

zōngfǎ 宗法

Feudal Clan System

中国古代以家族为中心，按血统、嫡庶来组织治理家族、国家、社会的原则和方法。宗法由父系氏族的家长制演化而来，定型于西周，与封建制等互为表里。宗法分为家国两个层面，在家的层面，宗族的嫡长子是家族的嫡系继承人，拥有家族的最高权力，其余家族成员依据亲疏、世系各自确定其在家族中的地位和权力。帝王公侯或者世家大族的宗族等级制扩展到国家的层面，对于王位继承与国家政治具有决定性的作用。宗法制数千年来对中国人的生活方式、思维方式影响深远。

This system was central to life in ancient China; it was a system of principles and measures by which a clan, a state, or society was run, based on bloodline or whether a son was born from the wife or a concubine. The feudal clan system evolved from the patriarchal chiefs system. Taking shape during the Western Zhou Dynasty, this system and the feudal system were mutually dependent and complementary. The feudal clan system had two levels: one was the familial level, where the eldest son by the wife was the first in line to inherit the family's property and thus enjoyed the greatest authority. Other members of the clan were allotted their status and authority according to their closeness of kinship, ancestry, or seniority. In the families of the emperor, kings, and other nobility, this pattern was extended to the state or national level. It had a decisive impact on the inheritance of the imperial throne and on state politics. The feudal clan system greatly influenced the Chinese way of life and thinking for several thousand years.

引例 Citation：

◎宗法者，佐国家养民教民之原本也。（冯桂芬《复宗法议》）
（所谓宗法，是帮助国家养育、教化民众的原始基础。）

The feudal clan system is a state's bedrock for fostering and educating its people. (Feng Guifen: My Argument for Restoring the Feudal Clan System)

术语表 List of Concepts

英文	中文
A Scabby Person and the Beautiful Lady Xishi Are the Same in the Eyes of Dao.	厉与西施，道通为一
A Single Note Does Not Compose a Melodious Tune, Nor Does a Single Color Make a Beautiful Pattern.	声一无听，物一无文
Ballad, Court Hymn, and Eulogy	风雅颂
Ben and *Mo* (The Fundamental and the Incidental)	本末
Charm of Spontaneity	自然英旨
Classical Academy	书院
Coexistence of All in Harmony	协和万邦
Constant Renewal	日新
Cultivate *Qi*	养气
Dao (Way)	道
De (Virtue)	德
Dependent Origination	缘起
Depressed and Enraged	悲慨
Direct Quest	直寻

英文	中文
Edify the Populace to Achieve a Harmonious Society	人文化成
Education for All Without Discrimination	有教无类
Embrace Distant Peoples by Means of Virtue	怀远以德
Express Enjoyment Without Indulgence and Express Grief Without Excessive Distress	乐而不淫，哀而不伤
Extolment and Satirical Criticism	美刺
Feudal Clan System	宗法
Feudal System / Feudalism	封建
Follow the Mandate of Heaven and Comply with the Wishes of the People	顺天应人
Form and Melody	格调
Gods of the Earth and the Five Grains / State / State Power	社稷
Governance Based on Virtue	为政以德
Heart / Mind	心
Highbrow and Lowbrow	雅俗
Huaxia / The Han People	华夏
Imaginative Contemplation	神思
Imperial Academy	太学
Indignation Spurs One to Write Great Works.	发愤著书

英文	中文
Kingly Way (Benevolent Governance)	王道
King	王
Latent Sentiment and Evident Beauty	隐秀
Li	理
Liangzhi (Conscience)	良知
Literature Is the Vehicle of Ideas.	文以载道
Make Full Use of Resources to Enrich the People	利用厚生
Narrative, Analogy, and Association	赋比兴
Naturalness	自然
Nine *Zhou* (Regions)	九州
Non-action	无为
Nuanced Flavor	滋味
People Are the Foundation of the State.	民惟邦本
Poetry Expresses Aspirations.	诗言志
Poetry Springs from Emotions.	诗缘情
Prajna / Wisdom	般若
Purple Prevailing over Red	紫之夺朱
Qi (Vital Force)	气
Qing	情

英文	中文
Qu	趣
Reasoning and Structure	肌理
Refining and Deleting	镕裁
Ren (Benevolence)	仁
Resonance and Empathy	知音
Righteousness	义
Rivers and Mountains / Country or State Power	江山
Rule by Law	法治
Rule by Man	人治
Sage / Sageness	圣
Select and Recommend	选举
Self-cultivation, Family Regulation, State Governance, Bringing Peace to All Under Heaven	修齐治平
Sentiment and Scenery	情景
Shaping the Mind Through Education	教化
Shen (Spirit / Spiritual)	神
Sincerity	诚
Stimulation, Contemplation, Communication, and Criticism	兴观群怨

英文	中文
Style and Temperament	体性
Subtle Admonition	讽谕
Taiji (The Supreme Ultimate)	太极
The Image Beyond an Image, the Scene Beyond a Scene	象外之象，景外之景
The Imperial Civil Examination System	科举
The One	一
The Six Basic Elements	六义
The Six Confucian Classics Are All About History.	六经皆史
Three Strengths of a Good Historian	史才三长
Ti and *Yong*	体用
Tian (Heaven)	天
Tianxia (All Under Heaven)	天下
Trustworthy Historian / Factual History	良史
Trustworthy Words May Not Be Fine-sounding; Fine-sounding Words May Not Be Trustworthy.	信言不美，美言不信
Universal Harmony	大同
Virtuous People Are Sure to Produce Fine Writing.	有德者必有言
Void and Peace	虚静

英文	中文
Wenming (Civilization)	文明
Wenqi	文气
Wu (Thing / Matter)	物
Wuxing	五行
Xing (Nature)	性
Xingling (Inner Self)	性灵
Xingxiang (Inspiring Imagery)	兴象
Xu (Void)	虚
Xuanlan (Pure-minded Contemplation)	玄览
Yin and Yang	阴阳
Yixiang (Imagery)	意象
You and *Wu*	有无
You Won't Be Able to Talk Properly with Others Without Studying *The Book of Songs*.	不学《诗》，无以言
Zhongguo (China)	中国
Zhonghua	中华
Zhongyong (Golden Mean)	中庸

中国历史年代简表 A Brief Chronology of Chinese History

夏 Xia Dynasty		2070-1600 BC
商 Shang Dynasty		1600-1046 BC
周 Zhou Dynasty		1046-256 BC
周 Zhou Dynasty	西周 Western Zhou Dynasty	1046-771 BC
	东周 Eastern Zhou Dynasty	770-256 BC
秦 Qin Dynasty		221-206 BC
汉 Han Dynasty		206 BC-AD 220
汉 Han Dynasty	西汉 Western Han Dynasty	206 BC-AD 25
	东汉 Eastern Han Dynasty	25-220
三国 Three Kingdoms		220-280
三国 Three Kingdoms	魏 Kingdom of Wei	220-265
	蜀 Kingdom of Shu	221-263
	吴 Kingdom of Wu	222-280
晋 Jin Dynasty		265-420
晋 Jin Dynasty	西晋 Western Jin Dynasty	265-317
	东晋 Eastern Jin Dynasty	317-420
南北朝 Southern and Northern Dynasties		420-589
南北朝 Southern and Northern Dynasties	南朝 Southern Dynasties	420-589
	南朝 Southern Dynasties — 宋 Song Dynasty	420-479
	齐 Qi Dynasty	479-502
	梁 Liang Dynasty	502-557
	陈 Chen Dynasty	557-589

南北朝 Southern and Northern Dynasties	北朝 Northern Dynasties		386-581
	北朝 Northern Dynasties	北魏 Northern Wei Dynasty	386-534
		东魏 Eastern Wei Dynasty	534-550
		北齐 Northern Qi Dynasty	550-577
		西魏 Western Wei Dynasty	535-556
		北周 Northern Zhou Dynasty	557-581
隋 Sui Dynasty			581-618
唐 Tang Dynasty			618-907
五代 Five Dynasties			907-960
五代 Five Dynasties	后梁 Later Liang Dynasty		907-923
	后唐 Later Tang Dynasty		923-936
	后晋 Later Jin Dynasty		936-947
	后汉 Later Han Dynasty		947-950
	后周 Later Zhou Dynasty		951-960
宋 Song Dynasty			960-1279
宋 Song Dynasty	北宋 Northern Song Dynasty		960-1127
	南宋 Southern Song Dynasty		1127-1279
辽 Liao Dynasty			907-1125
西夏 Western Xia Dynasty			1038-1227
金 Jin Dynasty			1115-1234
元 Yuan Dynasty			1206-1368
明 Ming Dynasty			1368-1644
清 Qing Dynasty			1616-1911
中华民国 Republic of China			1912-1949
中华人民共和国 People's Republic of China			Founded on October 1, 1949